June 2010
Carrie

Village Wisdom

Immersed in Uganda, Inspired by Job, Changed for Life

Story and Photographs by
Carrie Wagner

Published by Butler Mountain Press
129 Bleachery Blvd. #151
Asheville, NC 28805
First Edition

ISBN: 9780615346274
Printed in USA by RR Donnelly
Designer: Jamie Tomasi Bolak
Editor: Heather Jones

For those who follow their hearts...
Especially my husband Bob and my friend Job

and

For Adam and Benjamin, who have given me
an appreciation of God's magnificent love
through my love for them.

Writing and producing this book has been a challenging, but fulfilling journey.
The fulfillment rests in relationships with so many friends who have journeyed with
me, sharing their gifts of encouragement, technical expertise, financial support
and time. Heartfelt thanks to all of you who have made this book a reality.
This includes people and congregations from long ago who supported us during our
term of service in Uganda. It also includes hundreds of people who sponsored our
return trip to Uganda: folks from our *Covenant Community Church* family, friends in
our home town of Asheville and many more family and friends scattered throughout
the US, and countries beyond. I am also grateful to our friends in Uganda.
I cannot express in words the gratitude I feel for each and every person and the
special role you have played in bringing this vision to fruition.

CONTENTS

Foreword

The road to Ibanda is dusty and narrow as it winds through the Rwenzori foothills. Nearly eight hours earlier we had left Kampala, the bustling capital city of Uganda, and had already passed Queen Elizabeth National Park, where a herd of warthogs grazed near the highway. My visit to Ibanda was part of an extensive research trip for a book I wrote on Habitat for Humanity. I was seeking personal stories and the impact that Habitat had had on communities all over the world. As the road began to climb toward the snow-capped peaks, the third highest in Africa, I could see here and there the first hints of change in one of the poorest parts of the continent.

In the village of Ibanda, the people are subsistence farmers for the most part, raising just enough to feed themselves – with a little left over, if they are lucky, to sell at the market. Most are members of the Bakonzo tribe, whose population is split by Uganda's international border with the Congo. Back in 1991 a young white couple from North Carolina, Bob and Carrie Wagner, came to live among the Bakonzo, settling in at the trading center of Ibanda. The Wagners came on assignment from Habitat for Humanity International, having undertaken a three-year commitment to help oversee the building of houses.

By the time they left in 1994, Habitat houses had begun to dot the hillsides, their metal roofs glinting in the afternoon sun. When I visited the village in 1995, just a short time after the Wagners had gone, I discovered a legacy that seemed to go beyond those physical manifestations of progress. Bob and Carrie had spent months planting the seeds of the Habitat philosophy. Patiently they explained, again and again, the idea of building simple, decent and affordable houses, which homeowners could buy through no interest loans.

The house payments could then be used to pay for materials to build more homes. The cost of construction could be held down by people in the village working together, sharing the sweat and the joy that came with building a safe place to live.

During my visit to Ibanda, I spoke at length with Job Malighee, one of the local Habitat leaders. He was then a bright, articulate man of thirty-six, slender and unremarkable in his bearing, except for a smile that lit up the room. Job was delighted with the Habitat project. "When you work in partnership," he said, "it gets the work done faster than when you are alone. Bob and Carrie put people back in touch with something that was part of our culture in the past. When your coffee is ready to pick from the trees, you call your neighbor to assist you. That was how it was done in our grandfather's day."

This book, written, photographed and published by Carrie Wagner some fifteen years after she left Uganda, is a testament to the power of the Habitat ideal. But it is more than that. If the Wagners managed to leave in Ibanda a kind of blueprint for grassroots progress, the blueprint clearly went both ways. Bob and Carrie, as this book makes clear, were indelibly stamped by their time in the village. They remember with fondness their friends, including Job, whose wisdom they carried back to America.

They knew that the wisdom did not come easily. Uganda, through the years, had suffered massive human rights violations under Idi Amin, an eight-year period in which as many as a half million people were killed. In 1979, Amin was overthrown, but the killings continued until a new president, Yoweri Museveni, seized power in 1986 and brought a measure of stability to the country. Even so, the people in the mountains of Uganda were poor, and remain so today, living in villages where electricity and running water are scarce and where diseases like AIDS remain a crippling fact of daily life.

But the Wagners also found something else. There were habits and values among the village people that, while rooted in the reality of Third World poverty, offered inspiration to lands of greater abundance such as ours. There was, for example, a strong sense of community, the habit of neighbors to share what they had – joys, sorrows, food on the table – with each other, certainly, but also with visitors who might come along. The value of hospitality seemed to be universal, and if people often didn't have a lot to share, their lives, despite the hardships, seemed to be filled with a fundamental joy.

For the people of Ibanda, writes Carrie Wagner, "There is no such thing as living in isolation. When children are orphaned, they are taken in by extended family members. And because the Bakonzo people have been oppressed by other tribes and not even recognized officially … by the Ugandan government until recently, they have a strong sense of loyalty to each other. Their hardships, over centuries, have united them."

And it was also true that they never went hungry. Their land was fertile, and the temperate climate in the western highlands, so near the equator, allowed the fields to flourish year round. By the time the Wagners came to Ibanda, they found a people free from the devastations of hunger – so prevalent in other parts of the continent – and ready to try to build a better future.

Specifically, they were eager to build decent houses – to replace the thatched-roof huts with dirt floors and mud walls with sturdier dwellings of handmade brick.

Job Malighee embodied that hope. Like the biblical Job, he was a man of great faith who believed somehow that things would be better. He developed his own brick-making technology to supply the ingredients for Habitat houses, and he served as treasurer of the Habitat committee – less because of his bookkeeping skills than because everybody in the village seemed to trust him. And Job had other dreams as well. He knew the river that flowed by the village could become an angry torrent when it rained, sometimes sweeping people to their deaths.

The nearest bridge was a mile downstream, and Job set out to build one at Ibanda. It took him a decade to raise money for the project, but he never let go of that simple idea. There is a handsome photograph in this book of Job standing proudly beside the newly finished bridge, and it is part of the story that Carrie Wagner tells. Her photographs are a cornerstone of that telling, for in recent years photography has been her profession.

But it is also clear as the reader begins to leaf through the pages that this is much more than a picture book. It is a story fully told through the lens of Carrie's faith, which grew deeper during her years in Uganda. She saw in the lives of her friends in Ibanda a kind of perspective that she wanted for herself. In America, she writes, "Seeing 'more, more, more' promotes 'I want, I want, I want.' The cycle of poverty mirrors the cycle of materialism. Both revolve simultaneously, with little awareness of the other."

Carrie pulls no punches in telling her story. Through journal entries and letters back home, as well as her reflections of more recent years, she offers her "warts-and-all" account, describing, for example, the displacement she felt when she and Bob first came to Africa. For the Wagners, like others in their line of work, the exhilaration of a new adventure gradually, inexorably gave way to despair as they struggled to get Habitat off the ground. They learned the hard lessons of human nature as they encountered the feet of clay of their hosts.

But on the other side of those lessons, they came to love the people of Ibanda, to regard those friendships as some of the most important in their lives. They wept when their time in the village was up, but they also believed – more and more certainly as the years went by – that they would one day return.

Finally, in July of 2009, they set out once again from North Carolina, in the company this time of Adam and Benjamin, their two young sons. My wife Nancy and I were supposed to be with them, having planned to work with Carrie on the writing of this book. But as the day of our departure approached, a case of summer flu forced a change in our plans, and despite our disappointment at the time, I think that things worked out for the best.

This is a story that belongs to the Wagners, or at least in many ways that is true, for it is a deeply personal account. In the concluding chapters, Carrie tells of her family's return to Ibanda and the symbols of progress they saw all around – Job's bridge, the Habitat houses, the coffee cooperatives and soccer programs, the people with cell phones walking through the streets. But there were also some things that hadn't changed, chief among them the feelings of friendship and connection that had spanned the continents and the years.

This is the story of those connections, and as Carrie Wagner understands it, a story of global citizenship and finding a place in God's great world. It is a memoir offered with humility and heart, and for some of us lucky enough to read it, it carries a certain measure of discomfort. We are reminded of the magnitude of global need, and how little most of us do to meet it, and the opportunities we are missing in the process.

It may well be that the resulting unease is the greatest single gift of this book.

Frye Gaillard
December 2009

Frye Gaillard, writer in residence at the University of South Alabama, has written or edited more than twenty books, including *Cradle of Freedom: Alabama and the Movement That Changed America,* winner of the 2005 Lillian Smith Award for best southern non-fiction, and the 2007 non-fiction Book of the Year recognition from the Alabama Library Association. Gaillard's other award-winning books include *If I Were a Carpenter: Twenty Years of Habitat for Humanity; The Dream Long Deferred: The Landmark Struggle for Desegregation in Charlotte, North Carolina;* and *Watermelon Wine: The Spirit of Country Music.*

Dear Readers,

"Just build the houses, don't make too many waves, get to know the people and have fun. After it's all done, you can write a book about your experience." This was the advice given to my husband Bob and me by an expatriate development worker with 25 years experience living in Uganda. We had been in Uganda a year into our three-year term and were drowning in the swell of problems that churn the sea of poverty. We had read every book on rural development and had visited numerous other missions and development projects. It seemed the more we learned, the more questions we had, and the more hopeless we felt.

In the end, we heeded most of the expat's advice. Through a grueling cultural stripping process, we learned to let go of our Western ideals and appreciate the Ugandan people for who they are. We established a grassroots house-building model that involved many local people and our Habitat affiliate built 75 houses. But Bob and I did make waves about appropriate program implementation because we are both people of conviction. In the end, after we walked through the valley of darkness and crested the hump, we managed to have a lot of fun.

And now, 15 years after the experience, I am writing the book.

This book is divided into five sections, using a combination of stories and photographs to illuminate my literal and spiritual journey. The first section, "Transformation," sets the tone, defining transformation and addressing both the pain and joy inherent in this kind of all-encompassing change.

The section "Etchings" presents a collection of images culled from the hundreds of photographs I took in the village from 1991 to 1994. This collection of photographs is precious not only because of the personal nature of the portraits which were captured once I had built relationships, but also because of the high risk for damaged or lost film as it was transported from Africa to the United States.

"A Man Named Job" tells a bit of Job Malighee's story. Job, along with his biblical counterpart, was the central inspiration for my writing. This chapter also sheds light on the culture and environment of Job's tribe, the Bakonzo in western Uganda.

The heart of *Village Wisdom* is contained in the "Epiphanies" section. I chose the word "epiphany" to describe the lessons gained from my experiences, some of which were immediate revelations and others that have taken years to soak in. The stories are told through extracts of letters and journal entries that I wrote while we were there, followed by my current perspective on the experiences. While the stories are not linear or chronological, they are interwoven into a thematic structure.

"Uganda Revisited" tells the story of my 2009 return to Uganda, traveling with my husband and two young sons.

The "Afterword" is dedicated to the multitudes of people engaged in service, aiming to inspire continual stretch of personal boundaries and transformational life experiences.

The process of writing this book has been a transformational experience. I began to realize this when I was thick into salvaging memories and digging deep into thoughts and feelings about poverty, my place in the world and my spiritual journey. The commitment to thoroughly revisit (mentally, spiritually and physically) a place and time that had such impact on my life has been wearisome yet invigorating. I encourage you to revisit **your** places and experiences of transformation – and take the time to write about them.

Carrie Wagner
December 2009

Transformation

Though we often resist change, we seek to better ourselves, our communities and our world. The experiences that change our lives and transform our spirits are the very ones that have stripped us to nakedness, revealing our hearts, our insecurities and our dependence on others for survival.

Go to the people
Live with them
Love them
Learn from them
Work with them
Start with what they have
Build on what they know
And in the end
When the work is done
The people will rejoice:
"We have done it ourselves!"

Chinese Proverb

Journal Entry
March 1992

Crammed like sardines in a can, we sat "four, four" in the minivan, called a *matatu*. Matatus are the standard vehicles for public transportation from town to town. With four people on each bench seat and our bags stuffed between our feet, no one had any wiggle room. Bob and I were headed to Mbarara to meet with a new Habitat committee.

I had grown accustomed to tight seating arrangements. I was also used to two or three Ugandan dialects surrounding me, only understanding a few words here and there. The rhythm of start, speed, coast, stop - start, speed, coast, stop… had become natural for me, as this was our usual mode of transportation when going any further than Kasese town.

At each stop a new passenger got in and squeezed into the least crowded seat. Perhaps another passenger would offload, but not always. The new traveler would greet folks and sometimes spark conversation or laughter. Again, silence pervaded as we sped to the next stop, dodging potholes along the way. The door operator, who stood up or perched part of his bottom on a footstool next to the door, opened the side door when the matatu slowed to an almost but not complete stop. He collected 100 shillings from the passengers as they quickly boarded the coasting vehicle. And again: off, acceleration, speed, laughter, fading to silence.

We had made all of the stops and were settled in for about an hour's drive. The speed and bumpiness of the ride made it seem longer.

About halfway into the journey, we heard a loud bang – it sounded like a gunshot. When the matatu started wobbling uncontrollably, I knew that we had blown a tire. The driver was trying to hold the steering wheel steady as we coasted down from 100 kph. Even with the driver's best efforts, we were still wavering on and off the tarmac road.

I was seated by the window on the far left of the vehicle, so I could see all of the eucalyptus trees that we just missed. The colorful people and produce of the Ugandan countryside blended into an abstract painting as we sped past. For a brief moment, I thought of them and hoped that we would not hit anyone.

Then, I went selfishly internal, "This is it. We're all going to die. I'll never see my parents again. I'll never be a mother. This is the end for me."

In the same flash of a second, the woman seated beside me threw both of her arms into the air and began chanting, "Jesu, Jesu, Jesu." She was the only one who was not holding on to her seat or somebody else for dear life. I was squeezing the seat rail in front of me so tight that my knuckles turned white.

She did it again. Arms in the air, eyes closed, "Jesu! Jesu! Jesu!"

Suddenly we stopped. We were off the road and had landed in a clearing, free of trees, free of people, and free of houses.

Unbelievable.

Panic and relief filled the vehicle as we realized that all 17 of us had survived. We quickly climbed out of the minivan; we had survived the impact, but would the vehicle now blow up?

For the next couple of hours we waited on the side of the road for another public transport vehicle to pick us up – a few people at a time – there is no "call 911." We were at the mercy of other travelers who might stop to help us. Thankfully, there were no life-threatening injuries, although several passengers were experiencing shock.

I crawled inside of myself, tuning out all external stimuli, perhaps looking for Jesu. "Had he saved us? And if so, why? Was it because He was called?" I felt so terrible that I had not thought to call on Jesus. I had already declared my life over. I never even thought about Jesus. And here we had been spared, perhaps because of the woman who called "Jesu."

God, forgive me for neglecting to call on you. In a place where people truly rely on you for their daily bread, for your provision, protection and grace, help me to learn to do the same.

Training for Transformation, books 1, 2 and 3. If you have served with Peace Corps or other voluntary service organizations, you have probably studied these handbooks or other similar ones that are written for the community development worker. These handbooks are simple yet crucial guides to working with the poor and oppressed. Extremely relevant for our work in Africa, we followed many of the procedures and activities, integrating them with practices from local development initiatives. I also used these books to train international volunteers who would be working in similar circumstances around the world with Habitat for Humanity International.

There is an irony. Transformation in these books refers to changes for community. The field guides are about empowering indigenous folks to address their own problems, discussing and designing creative solutions rather than sinking into unhealthy dependency models of top-down development. What I did not realize during my 11 years with Habitat for Humanity International is that the real transformation would take place in me – that my years in Uganda and South Africa and the many years that I worked in the international development and training realm, were in fact, "Training for my own Transformation."

To transform is to change into something different, to take on a new form or shape. People speak of "life changing" experiences. Those can be as brief as a near-death car accident or a fright that challenges one's immortal perspective, or even a mission trip. Other life changing experiences are long-term commitments that involve sacrifice: marriage, parenting, career change, and chronic illness.

The transformations I describe in this book refer to change of heart, perspective, worldview and values. When sojourners return from overseas living,

their loved ones at home may notice some changes in physical appearance or behaviors. What is not so obvious is the internal transformation that has occurred. Even the sojourner is sometimes unaware of the transformation. He/she feels the emotions associated with the transformation and often settles for an "I don't fit in anywhere" attitude.

When we returned from Uganda, I knew I had changed. I went through the typical re-entry process, which is often referred to as reverse culture shock. Actually, re-entry follows the same pattern as cultural adaptation to a foreign country. It begins with the honeymoon stage where everything is new and exciting and all opportunities are welcome adventures. Then, anxiety and hostility set in as the sojourner feels isolated and judged by host country nationals. Over time, after the person has engaged in meaningful activities and relationships, he adjusts and most likely achieves cultural adaptation. By this stage, the individual has become a blended, multi-cultural being.

To my benefit, following our term of service, I continued working with Habitat for Humanity International. In my job as an international trainer, I studied and taught about culture shock and the cultural adaptation process. My co-workers had all lived overseas. I was immersed in a community of people who understood me, unlike others who return to their home feeling alienated because their loved ones do not understand the internal turmoil experienced when readjusting from third world conditions to first world environments.

As I look through my journal of the year following my three years in Uganda, my focus seemed to be relearning to cope in American society. The skills I had developed in order to survive in Africa were irrelevant back at home (or so I thought). My frame of reference was different and the only emotion I could describe was numbness. This numbness lasted for quite some time, and had I not been in an environment where I had the freedom to discuss re-entry issues with people who cared, it might have taken much longer.

Though I knew I had changed, I did not know how those changes would be reflected in my life or what it really meant. As I spent the following years training and preparing international partners to go out and "do Habitat" in over 50 countries, being able to tell them anything beyond, "It will change your life forever," was out of my realm of certainty. I knew the cultural adaptation process well – lived it, studied it, taught it over and over. There is no doubt that living overseas is a transformative endeavor. Defining the transformation itself is a task that needn't be conquered by every sojourner, but one that I am compelled to complete.

To fully describe a transformation, perhaps it is necessary to depict the before and after. If you knew me before and after, the transformation might not be obvious. It would be easier to describe a transformation that took on more outward signs. "I quit smoking" or "I lost 150 pounds" or "I stopped gambling." No, my transformation was an internal evolution that happened so slowly that many of the implications of the changes are still being realized as my life unfolds.

When I left for Uganda, I was already a committed Christian. Perhaps my faith took on new challenges, but in the end it was ever strengthened. I was a motivated, creative being, always dreaming up new projects to carry out my lofty ideals and goals. I had married the man of my dreams and was determined to keep God at the center of our marriage. My idea of a perfect day included pancakes for breakfast in bed, a hike in a beautiful setting, a second cup of coffee and a piece of chocolate after lunch, a run or some tennis with Bob, and cooking a delicious gourmet dinner at home while listening to Joni Mitchell or James Taylor on the stereo.

Fast forward 18 years. My personal description echoes the same characteristics and interests; only now my perfect day also includes enjoying the activities that our two sons bring into the mix. So, what changed?

A simple, yet complex explanation includes becoming a "global citizen" – taking on a worldview that is outward, rather than ethnocentric. I realize that not everyone has the desire or the opportunity to travel and develop a love for diversity; however, those who do share a common ground – an indefinable place that has no borders. I am naturally drawn to other global citizens. Not because I seek them out; somehow they naturally cross my path. And it is often months into a friendship before I realize that a new friend has also experienced cross-cultural immersion. The attraction to other sojourners is like the relationships among other groups of people. For instance, motherhood; once you become a mother, you have a certain affinity and understanding for other mothers in the world. Motherhood encompasses a love and sense of responsibility that is inexplicable. Moms can simply look at each other and experience a comforting, "I know" or "I understand," just through a hug of the eyes.

This sense of "I know" transpires between global citizens as well. The shared values of global citizens cross political, religious, regional and generational borders. And though everyone's experience is unique and filtered through their own set of beliefs, common threads unite the overseas sojourners. Each has, through testing and trying times, become multicultural. They have picked up some traditions, habits and culture-specific behaviors from another place in the world and have molded them into their own personal palette. They have taken on a genuine respect and appreciation for diversity, recognizing that there are pros and cons to all cultures. Most importantly, each sojourner has a little pocket of her heart filled with someone far away – a person or a community who has helped shape her very soul.

Total immersion, living within another culture or part of the world, brings about life-long transformation. It enhances understanding of one's own culture and home country while boosting commitment to global issues. Global citizenship does not rival patriotism. It simply means thinking beyond one's own country and making lifestyle choices that promote a "win" for everyone.

As I think of Job and many other villagers whom we grew so fond of, the people who took us into their community and melded us into their lives, I attribute leaps of personal growth to examples set by them. They knew not, nor did I, how their simple lifestyle and the friendships that we shared would continually shape the lives of Bob and Carrie Wagner, and eventually the Wagner children.

Etchings

Photographs by Carrie Wagner

Some images remain etched in your heart forever. I discovered this as I dusted off the 15-year-old negatives of our time living in Uganda. I realized that though they have been packed away in notebooks for years, the images are just as vivid in my mind as they were when I experienced the moments. I also discovered that these images are timeless. While they represent a place and time, as all photographs do, on a broader scale they speak about the incredible richness of life that co-exists with poverty environments. Our assumptions about impoverished conditions are challenged as we witness joy, community and simplicity in the lives of those who have not been consumed by the material world. Children laugh and play; people work hard to sustain life; they help each other build; they socialize at the markets; they eat together and tell stories for entertainment.

These portraits represent the Bakonzo tribe in western Uganda. The Bakonzo live on the steep slopes of the Rwenzori Mountains, often referred to as "Mountains of the Moon." This collection of images, selected from hundreds of negatives shot during 1991-1994, portrays village life. As you look into these faces, I hope you see pride, strength and a willingness to share.

I remember my first experience aiming a camera at an Ugandan woman, deep in the mountains. As I gasped at the horror in her face, Job our Ugandan host said, "She doesn't want you to take her picture. People here believe that you are stealing their soul into the camera." I put the camera away and waited nearly a year before photographing people. Once I had built trust and personal relationships, the camera ceased to be an obstacle and I was able to capture the beauty of life in rural Uganda with integrity and authenticity.

Many years later, I came to realize that the woman was right. Making photographic portraits is taking a little piece of an individual's soul. Authentic portraiture requires a level of trust. When people "let me in" I am able to capture a sense of their spirit, whether it's through their eyes, their actions or their expressions. I have not in fact stolen their soul; rather, they have given a piece of it. I am honored to present these portraits because I believe that they honor the true givers.

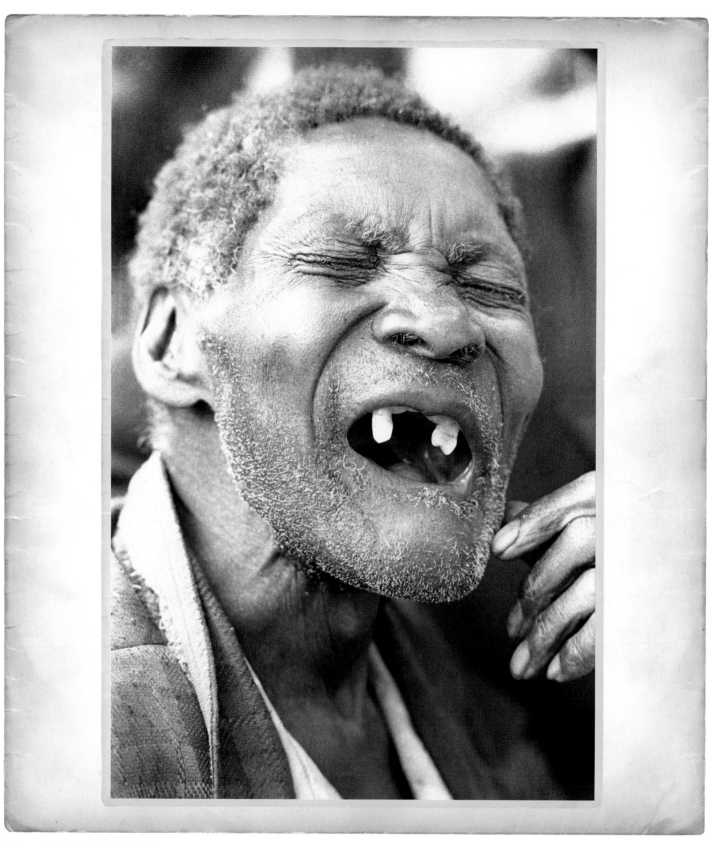

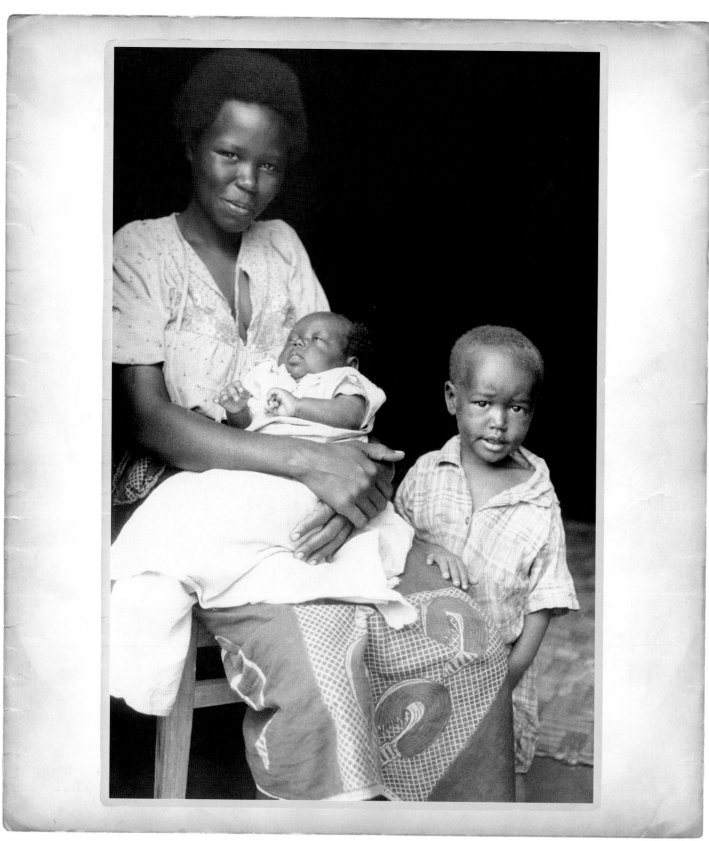

The Story Behind the Negatives

Perhaps the history of these images is one of the most significant aspects of the collection, especially as I have preserved them in the digital era where instant gratification abounds in all arenas.

There were many opportunities for these images to get spoiled by humidity or lost en route. There was no easy way to process the film. We lived in a rural area that didn't have running water or electricity. While I knew I could get marginal-quality color prints done in the city of Kampala (8 hours away), there was nowhere to develop black-and-white film. The postal system in Uganda was not reliable. In fact, in addition to several lost packages addressed to us, the box of books that we had mailed to ourselves before departing the states arrived in Uganda after we had returned to the states following our 3 year term of service.

In order to reduce the risk of losing film, I gave a couple of rolls at a time to European or American tourists (many of them strangers to us and often at their offer to cover the mailing costs), and once they returned to their home, they would mail them to Byron Baldwin in Charlotte, NC, who had agreed to process the film. Byron, my high school photography teacher, together with his students, developed over 40 rolls of film over that three year period and sent contact sheets to me in Uganda. To my knowledge, not one of them was lost.

All images were shot on Kodak TRI-X 400 film with a Nikon FM 35 mm camera. I learned through the fogginess of some images that my camera had been growing a fungus. Thankfully this did not destroy all images.

The film was scanned at 4000 DPI and in addition to the reproductions in this book, the images are displayed in a traveling photography exhibit, called *Portraits of Uganda.*

A Man Named Job

Confined by boundaries of poverty, Job lives a faithful life following dreams, seeking truth and serving others. He demonstrates grace, humility, patience and perseverance – characteristics that are more likely given than earned. Or, perhaps these qualities come through struggle, hard work and loss. Whatever the source, Job's character is admirable and inspiring. I write about Job with utmost respect and gratitude, both virtues I learned by living near Job in western Uganda.

"Let's try here," he said. Job walked through the tall grass with confidence, periodically checking behind to see if we were still close at foot. "There are some large rocks here. We should be able to cross." Job stepped up to the edge of the river and pointed to stones poking through the steady flow of white water. "I will help you," he said in response to my troubled expression.

Then he studied his route for just a moment, nodded his head and smiled, "Yeah, let's cross." Before he had gained our consent, Job was rolling up his pant legs, and removing his shoes. "Let me first take your bag and camera across safely. Then I'll come back for you." Job reached out his hand for my most treasured possession.

After taking our things across, Job helped me and Bob, one by one, to cross the river. He thought it funny that we would leave on our shoes (Teva® sandals) in the river.

Holding on to Job's hand only in a couple of tricky spots, Bob crossed first and rolled his pant legs back down when he reached the other side. I, on the other hand, clung to Job's hand the whole crossing, lifting and bunching my skirt just above my knees with the other hand. Job's gentle guidance and patience eased my timidity. "Put your foot there," he said, pointing to a submerged rock. And then we both laughed at my hesitant step and at the children who surrounded us, watching with delight.

We, the *bazungu* (white people) frequently provided regular entertainment for the whole village. "They are just curious," Job would say, wanting to protect us from feeling ridiculed. Then he would politely greet the children and suggest that they go back to their classrooms.

Job Malighee. (Jōb Maa lee ay). His name, like all names in the Bakonzo tribe, has significant meaning. In *Lukonzo*, Job's language, Malighee means "the one who carries sorrow." Job's mother told him when he was a young boy that he was unlucky to be born alone, with no siblings to share responsibilities and burdens. Job's mother died when he was young – "around 12 years old," he says. A few years later his father also passed away. Job does not know the particulars about either of the deaths, and since Job was an only child, he was left with no one to share the sorrow. After grieving the deaths of his parents, Job gave himself the name Malighee.

In the Bakonzo culture, which has adapted to the rugged environment of remote steep mountains, daily life hosts numerous hardships.

People die of unknown causes. The pain and disappointment of losing parents, siblings, children or other loved ones is bottled and capped. To talk much about it or research the causes of death brings sorrow to the survivors and disrespect to the deceased. Therefore, the Bakonzo accept their fate and move on. Job was, however, thankful for the love and care that his mother had given him. "I thank my mother, who shaped and guided me, otherwise when a person faces such problems he ends up drinking beer to forget his sorrows."

Job Malighee is one of the two Jobs I know. I know the other Job only through his story in the Bible. And though we don't know the author of his written story nor whether Job was a man or a figure representing a community over a span of years (there are different theories and interpretations of the biblical account), the biblical Job's story is a powerful one. After coming to know Job Malighee, I spent time coming to know the biblical Job because I sensed parallels in their characters, their hardships, and their persistence of faith. It is these parallels that have lured me into the quest of studying their personal stories, searching for the spiritual lessons embodied in each. The lives of Job Malighee and the community he represents are at the core of this book.

Job Malighee lives in the Rwenzori Mountains of western Uganda. These majestic mountains are home to thousands of Bakonzo people. Bakonzo, meaning "mountain people," is but one of over thirty tribes and languages of Uganda. And, like many other African tribes, the Bakonzo were split by national borders created by the British and the Belgians. The border between Uganda and the Democratic Republic of Congo runs along the ridges and peaks of the Rwenzori Mountains. Thus, over half of the Bakonzo live in Congo, while the rest of them live in Uganda. While Congo has undergone much influence from Belgium colonization, and likewise, Uganda from British, the language and culture of the Bakonzo has remained intact. Clan and family ties are strong – even across the national border.

At five feet, eight inches, with a slender physique, Job appears taller than the average *mukonzo* (person from the Bakonzo tribe). Typically the Bakonzo are short, stocky, and strongly equipped to handle mountainous terrain.

With broad flat noses and dark, but not black skin tones, their features are easily distinguishable from other Ugandan tribes. Except for his additional height, Job carries the characteristics of a mukonzo, especially in his ever-present smile.

In spite of tribal history marked with turbulence and oppression, the Bakonzo are happy people who enjoy talking and laughing. Their full lips frame big white teeth. And even the mouths that have lost a few teeth to poor hygiene still portray the warmth and welcome that invites strangers and loved ones alike. To the visitor, the joyous nature of the people contradicts the immense poverty conditions that define their lifestyle.

I first met Job in 1991, the initial year of a three-year span that my husband Bob and I lived in Uganda. A twenty-something-year-old newlywed with ambition and good intentions, I entered Uganda as a sponge, filling all senses with the mystiques of a foreign land.

Job, 32 years old at the time, was one of many local Habitat for Humanity committee members whom we met during our whirlwind tour of western Uganda, where we had been assigned as International Partners. When we were given the assignment after three months of training at Habitat for Humanity International (HFHI) headquarters, I had imagined moving to a small village, immersing ourselves into the culture and working with a group of community-elected committee members. But unfortunately, Bob and I were stationed in Kasese town, which is central to many rural mountainous villages that made up the Rwenzori Habitat affiliate. Therefore, our visits to each village, like Ibanda and Kyanya, (where Job lives) were brief and quite superficial.

Relying on our intuition to sense people of good character and integrity, we spent months feeling disappointed and frustrated with most of the committee members from the Habitat projects. Our Western concept of volunteerism clashed with the reality of communities where almost everyone is in need of better housing. We found mostly HFH committee members who were seeking to serve themselves and some who were clever enough to divert project funds for personal endeavors, unrelated to house building.

The corruption which entwines impoverished societies is among the initial shocks for expatriates. In the beginning, when the sojourner is inexperienced and harbors naïve hopes and expectations, corruption seems black and white. Slowly, through years of living and studying the influences of socio-economic dynamics, she begins to understand the layers of complexity. Since I was young in my community development experience, it was solely my intuition that guided me to believe that Job was a man of good principles and genuine in his desire to help his community.

It was a year later that I would come to know Job personally. Bob and I were given the chance to choose a village in which to reside and work with one branch of the Rwenzori Habitat project. We were given freedom to pilot a grassroots program, structured differently than Habitat's traditional model. We chose to move to Ibanda. Job was among others on the committee there whom we felt drawn to. We moved to the Ibanda trading center in 1992, and focused on just two out of the eight sub-counties that made up Rwenzori Habitat. Our new community and surrounding mountain villages were overjoyed that we had selected them to live and work with.

The dirt road to Ibanda climbs fifteen kilometers through the Mobuku Valley, nestled in the foothills of the Rwenzori Mountains, and ends at the base of Rwenzori National Park. The rocky road, wide enough for only one car in some stretches, is bordered most of the way by banana trees, coffee plantations and other farmland. There is a steady stream of people moving up and down, (on foot) carrying water, or sacks of produce on their heads and backs. Some herd goats and cattle. The primitive lifestyle and lack of development somehow contribute to the beauty of the land. Human life is so dependent on and integrated with the environment that the two weave a common tapestry.

Ibanda is a trading center located more than halfway up the length of the road. Besides having a few shops and a crossroad corner where a small market unfolds once a week, Ibanda trading center is the place where the views of snow-capped peaks begin. The road beyond Ibanda climbs steadily towards the 16,000 foot peaks, offering spectacular scenery and awe-inspiring views.

Children along the road stop walking as vehicles pass. They wave and spread big smiles, saying "*Mzungu*, (white person) how are you?" Many white people pass through the Mobuku valley on their way to climb the mountain peaks, the third highest in Africa. But few have taken the time to befriend the Bakonzo. As it turned out, we were among a handful of *bazungu* (white people) who would ever spend extended time with these people, in this part of the district. (Missionaries, development workers and foreign medical staff have a scattered presence throughout Kasese District.)

Gracefully winding its way through the valley is the Mobuku River, the primary water source for thousands of people. Women and children carry water from the river to their homes on a daily basis, some walking several kilometers uphill.

Ibanda Habitat was designed to assist villages and home sites on both sides of the river. When Bob and I moved to Ibanda, we were not aware of the vastness of the area we would cover on foot and how skilled we would become at river crossing. We were also not aware of Job's vision to build a bridge that would safely connect the communities residing on both sides of the river. As we came to know and love Job, we witnessed his passion for community service, not only through his dedication to the Habitat project but also through his countless hours of preparing proposals for building a bridge – a venture that would end up taking ten years to come to fruition.

Most of the houses in this area were made of mud and wattle (reeds tied together for structure) and had poorly thatched grass roofs. It was common for a family of nine or ten to live in a 300-square-foot house, sharing two bedrooms and one common sitting room. In Bakonzo culture, kitchens and "boy's quarters" are housed in a separate building at the back of the main house. Boys move out of the main house around age 13, even though they come into manhood by circumcision at age 18. Cooking on an open fire is the norm, which makes for very smoky kitchens. I would politely greet the women while they were cooking, but then quickly bow out, as I couldn't handle the smoke in my eyes.

The housing conditions in Ibanda and surrounding communities fit Habitat's qualifications of "substandard" and the local people had written an impressive proposal for assistance. There was no doubt that these communities would benefit from better building technologies and more durable construction, and of course, loans for affordable house construction.

Job was among the original Habitat committee members who wrote the proposal. But more remarkable than his involvement with Habitat was his initiation of a brick making project. Having learned the brick making technology from builders in Kasese town, Job piloted this new technique in his village. Job's brick project made quite an impression upon us on our initial visit to the area.

Perhaps the most poignant truth about this

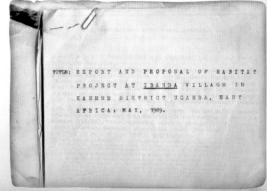

culture residing on mountain slopes and in the valley that lies between is the subsistence lifestyle. The Bakonzo people are farmers who cultivate the families' annual food from their steep unterraced land. They travel on foot, (often in bare feet), carrying heavy loads on their backs, up and down the mountains. While men help prepare the soil, women do most of the farming; they dig, plant, cultivate and occasionally take excess food to sell at the market. The men are responsible for building the house and looking for income. Few people have jobs: the public transport drivers, shop owners, and those who have positions with the government or development agencies like Habitat. Most families struggle to generate income, and even if the husband has a job, it does not provide enough income to pay for school fees and medical care.

Even though there is a power station near Ibanda, there has been so little development over the years that only a handful of homes have electricity. The power generated through the plant is exported to other parts of Uganda. People living near and far from the power plant are living in darkness, cooking with firewood and doing all household chores by hand. The year-round moderate temperatures and the lack of services from the government have contributed to the continuation of subsistence living.

One of the beauties embedded in the Bakonzo culture is their sense of community. They share everything: food, joys, sorrows, child rearing, and the responsibility for improvement of life conditions. There is no such thing as living in isolation. When children are orphaned, they are taken in by extended family members. And because the Bakonzo people have been oppressed by other tribes and not recognized officially as a kingdom by the Ugandan government until recently, they have a strong sense of loyalty to each other. Their hardships, over centuries, have united them.

Though subsistence farming is challenging, the land in western Uganda is fertile. Food grows all year long. People are not starving.

They grow what they need on their own land and some also grow cash crops, like coffee. The simplicity of this lifestyle has its appeal to Westerners who come from cold climates. But the appeal is weakened when one realizes that basic needs like housing, clean water, medical care, and education are not being met. Commodities and services that require money, if only a little, are not obtained because people simply do not have money. The lack of income generation illuminates the contrast between the richness of culture and the problems of poverty – a dichotomy I have struggled with for 18 years now. Development is certainly double-edged.

Life struggles have also made the Bakonzo a spiritual people. Though their traditional beliefs include multiple gods and witchcraft, (beliefs that conflict with monotheism) faith in a higher power is and has always been core to their survival. While some are Muslims, the majority of Bakonzo are Christians who read the Bible regularly and rely on God for protection, provision and deliverance.

Ever since he was a young adult, Job has attended the Seventh Day Adventist Church (SDA) and has relied on his faith in God. He credits his mother for instilling good values in him. When Job was young, his mother told him "to be obedient and faithful…the world is round my son, you don't know who shall help you."

Job's parents were Catholic, but as a lone seeker, Job found the SDA beliefs to fit his search. The Bible, the only formal book translated into Lukonzo, has been a source of inspiration for Job. He reads his Bible daily and often carries it with him. Job's favorite scripture is John 3:16, "For God so loved the world that he gave his one and only Son, that whoever believes in him shall not perish but have eternal life."

Job's uncle, who had taken responsibility for paying Job's school fees after Job's father died, also passed away, leaving Job with no family or support. Job was in Primary Seven (P7) at the time, and though the government under President Obote's regime allowed orphans to study for free, that privilege was soon taken away by a new government. Thus, Job had no means of furthering his education. Job had already become an astute reader and has always treasured his ability to communicate through the written word. While many of Job's peers went on to finish higher grade levels, Job made the most of his limited schooling, using creative thinking skills, compassion and perseverance to organize the community to solve problems.

But Job's cleverness is not what has drawn me into his life and his story. So what is it about Job? Why is his character of such value to me?

I'll start with his charm. Job is a good-looking man, unbeknownst to himself, who reveals a gentle manner through his interactions. We worked together on Habitat accounting and project organization. He visited us almost daily for two years, teaching me and Bob the language (Lukonzo) and guiding us through the culture. Together we laughed at cultural differences, mutually appreciating the value of cross-cultural friendship. Job often smiled, and listened with his eyes, seeming to ponder our words long after they were spoken. Job is quick to laugh and unafraid to show compassion. He is a likeable guy.

I remember Job mostly in two sets of clothes: his tattered work clothes, which he wore while farming and brick making, and his neat and tidy "smart casual" attire, which he wore in public, away from his home compound. When away from home, Job dressed in a pair of clean, lightly pressed (coal-heated iron), trousers with a leather belt and a button-up short-sleeved shirt. His style was appropriate for the warm temperatures, but also indicative that he cared about his appearance. During rainy seasons, when temperatures were a little cooler, he often wore a red blazer.

For me, Job's trademark was his hat. More often than not, he wore a tan cloth hat that I have always thought of as his Gilligan hat. (Yes, I grew up watching *Gilligan's Island* on TV.)

Perhaps Job's charm is a bonus to the qualities that have put him on the cover of this book. That he is a common villager with only seven years of education and struggling through the hardships of poverty is significant. God uses ordinary people to set examples. Unlike the biblical Job, whose wealth and family were stripped from him through a series of personal calamities, Job Malighee has never experienced wealth, political highness or wide-spread recognition. (I think he has only been to the capital city of Kampala twice). He is a peasant farmer, like his neighbors. Rooted in Bakonzo culture, he is proud of his traditions, which have been passed down for many generations. With delight, Job demonstrates how to eat *obundu* (staple food made from cassava flour) and how to show respect for elders.

Job's hardships are not unique. They are common to people in his community. Job and his family have, through many years, suffered from bouts of malaria, miscarriages, and kidney disease. During five years of rebel activity, (1996-2001) a tumultuous time for all mountain dwellers, Job suffered from headache and mental instability. Some residents who lived higher in the mountains were even forced from their homes. Job remained in his home but his mental instability caused him to refrain from all physical labor. Job describes his illness, "I was unable to dig, or make bricks or do anything. Eventually, I recovered."

Job continued having children with his wife and ended up with six, five girls who followed his firstborn male, Jahard. Job has always struggled to afford basic family needs – decent housing, primary education for his kids, and medical care. Providing for his wife and children is his utmost priority. The challenge to meet basic needs is not unique to Job; it is a struggle widespread among the Bakonzo.

The uniqueness of Job – and consistent with the traits of the biblical Job – is his unwavering faith in God, through the good and bad times, even at the expense of being ridiculed by his peers.

Job's faith has given him the patience and perseverance necessary for seeing his hopes and dreams realized. Job is a visionary man and has been the catalyst for several community development projects. At a time when all of his neighbors lived in mud and wattle houses, Job was entrepreneurial in bringing a brick-making technology to the village. When he first started the brick project on his land, neighbors laughed at him and told him he was wasting his time and energy. Incidentally, fifteen years later, his neighbors and others in nearby communities, live in houses constructed from his bricks.

Another project spearheaded by Job was the construction of a bridge across the Mobuku River. The completion of the bridge happened ten years after we left

Ibanda, but we kept up with the progress through Job's letters to us through the years. It took 12 years to secure funding and build the bridge. Job began fundraising for the bridge in 1995, starting with a letter to us and our network of supporters. The $8,000 we raised was a good start for the bridge, but all construction and development efforts came to a halt during the years of political instability. Shortly thereafter, and when Job had healed from his illness, he continued his efforts of mobilizing the community. He also applied to numerous organizations for additional funding. With the aid of a French mining company and the Ugandan government, a bridge capable of supporting heavy vehicles was completed. The bridge turned out far superior to the footbridge Job had originally planned.

Among Job's attributes that have put him in community leadership roles is his trustworthiness. Having seen the level of responsibility required for managing Habitat funds, we were at first surprised that the Ibanda committee had not chosen a person with higher education credentials to handle the money. It became clear to us within a matter of weeks that Job was selected to be treasurer of the project because he had proven his integrity.

On a continent where corruption easily seeps into business, faith-based or otherwise, being chosen to account for finances is a great honor. And Job's diligence in learning the skills of budgeting, bookkeeping and inventory management demonstrated his desire to be effective in his role. Bob and I enjoyed teaching Job basic double-entry bookkeeping, a set of skills that he treasures to this day.

When asking other people, "What do you appreciate about Job?" I consistently get answers like, "He is kind." "He is a man of principles." "He is gentle." "He is trustworthy." These virtues sound awfully biblical to me. In Galatians 5:22, the apostle Paul gives a list of "fruits of the spirit" and contrasts them with "deeds of the flesh" (Galatians 19-20.) The love, joy, peace, patience, kindness, goodness, faithfulness, gentleness and self-control described by Paul are qualities resulting from seeds planted by the Holy Spirit. They are not rewards for good deeds. Even church critics or people from other faiths would find these qualities alluring. The spiritual fruits (blessings) that shape Job's actions are genuinely sacred.

For one who had spent such little time in the Bible during my childhood and adolescence, I knew enough about the biblical Job to recognize some irony in Job Malighee's name.

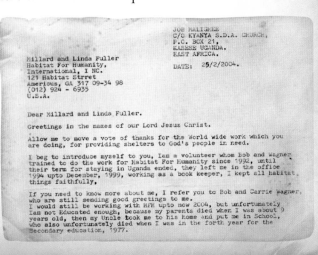

We would often say that "our Habitat Job has the patience of Job" – an expression well known by Christians. And, when Job came to us with problems of sickness, I thought about the suffering of the biblical Job. But it was years later that I would take the time to study him. Reading the Old Testament is drudgery for me, the pacifist who more readily gravitates to the hope, grace and forgiveness that came through Jesus and the Holy Spirit. I like the Jesus stories.

Then one day, I got it. Without the history of the fall of man, the holy wars, the testing of faiths, the prophets and the religious laws –the New Testament would have little relevance. The birth, life, death and resurrection of Jesus would be less meaningful.

The book of Job in the Bible, as well as other Old Testament stories, is indeed a prerequisite for understanding the good news of the gospels. And after better understanding the biblical Job's story, I was able to see far more than parallels to Job Malighee's character. I see ways in which the Holy Spirit has worked in his life, and similarly, in my own.

Job Malighee is not the biblical Job. He's not Jesus. And he's probably not the superman I have painted him to be. He is an ordinary man, yet one of my personal heroes. As you get into my story, you will get plenty of negative scoop – it's straight from my heart – the good, the bad and the ugly. But digging up dirt on Job to prove his authenticity doesn't feel necessary to me. He's a good man and certainly represents a place and time in our lives that planted lifelong seeds for transformation.

Job is not the only one from Uganda who impacted our lives. We think of many others – Bwanandeke, Kumaraki and Ellen, Mugisha and Betty, Kikundi Nelson, Joy Mubunga, Stanley Masereka, Stephen and Grace Masereka, Baita Francis, Edward Baringa, Donalt, Bongeri, and many others – who continue to hold their special place in our hearts. All of these friends, from such a beautiful culture in a beautiful land, deserve recognition and heartfelt thanks for sharing their lives with us.

I will never admit your are in the right; till I die, I will not deny my integrity

Job 27:5

Epiphanies

The following chapters are my Epiphany Chapters. I have chosen the word epiphany to represent the lessons learned from living in the village. The story unfolds in these chapters thematically, not chronologically.

Epiphany, defined in *The American Encarta Dictionary*: 1) A sudden realization, a sudden intuitive leap of understanding, especially through an ordinary but striking occurrence. 2) Appearance of God, the supposed manifestation of a divine being.

My epiphanies encompass the "Village Wisdom" gained through immersing ourselves in Ibanda and from the cross-cultural relationships we have maintained over the 15 years following our stay. They are the "Ah-ha's," the light switches in our heads, the twinges of pain and joy that have left marks on our hearts.

While many of the epiphanies were instant revelations, others have taken years to process and understand. For me, these epiphanies have become words to live by. And though the lessons are not based on specific biblical scripture, they demonstrate Jesus' teachings and other biblical stories. They also reflect core values of other religions and world cultures.

My epiphanies have become the framework, within our Christian context, for our family life. They are principles that we teach our kids, realizing that we teach best by modeling our beliefs. We hope and pray that the seeds planted will be nurtured by our children's own experiential learning.

Epiphany Chapters

> *Simple, Decent and Affordable*
> *Trash and Treasure*
> *My Life of Luxury*
> *My Life of Job*
> *Authentic Friendship*
> *Judgment*
> *Peace that Passes Understanding*
> *Seasons*

Immersion

One can only begin to understand another by walking
in his shoes. It is human nature to judge others out of our own ignorance.
Therefore, immerse yourself fully into whatever it is you wish to understand.

The seven hour drive back to Charlotte was both an eternity and a blink. I knew Bob was also replaying the interview we had had with the Africa Area Director for Habitat for Humanity International.

"We would like to volunteer for one year," said Bob very nobly to the area director.

"Well, that's great; however, we do not have a short term volunteer program anymore. The International Partner program is a three year commitment. You will live and work in a rural area, and work with local leadership to develop an appropriate, sustainable house building program."

He continued, "You will live as the people live, no running water or electricity. You will eat what they eat, learn their language and adapt to a very simple lifestyle. It is a challenging assignment, yet one that can offer lifelong fulfillment. Oh, and we suggest that you do not come home during that time. Habitat will not pay for a return trip until the end of your three year term. We have found that when overseas volunteers return home, even for a short visit, they quickly become disillusioned and struggle to complete their term of service."

We sat in silence for the entire drive. The weight of the interview was too heavy to spark any conversation between Bob and me. All I could think was, Three years!??! Three years. Three years!??!??! Live in the African bush for three years? Is he crazy?

We broke our silence with an outburst of laughter as we read the graffiti painted in big red letters on an overpass bridge. "TRUST JESUS."

"What are you thinking?" asked Bob in a gentle whispery kind of voice. "Well, I think we should trust Jesus," I replied with a bit of sarcasm but genuine heart. For us, making this decision did mean trusting Jesus, in a way that we had never been challenged to do before. To immerse ourselves, our lives and our hearts into another place, people and culture for three years was an act of faith as well as a leap into our desire for shared adventure.

Each one should use whatever gift he has received to serve others, faithfully administering God's grace in its various forms.

1 Peter 4:10

Journal Entry

July 1991

Our initial journey to Kasese town, where we will live for the first part of our term, was by way of pickup truck. There was enough room for us in the cab of the truck, but our co-workers who would be serving in Kasese District as well, rode in the back, surrounded by sacks of food and staple supplies, several suitcases and a trunk of our personal belongings. It was the longest trip of my life (so far).

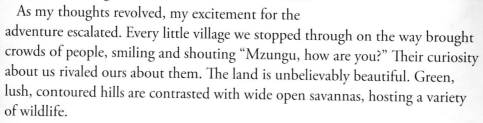

My mind circled. "Three years. Middle of nowhere. Can't speak the language. Do I have enough tampons? Will I get malaria? Have to boil the water."

As my thoughts revolved, my excitement for the adventure escalated. Every little village we stopped through on the way brought crowds of people, smiling and shouting "Mzungu, how are you?" Their curiosity about us rivaled ours about them. The land is unbelievably beautiful. Green, lush, contoured hills are contrasted with wide open savannas, hosting a variety of wildlife.

We arrived at our new home, tired from the journey and our senses overwhelmed with data. Ellen, Karen and David were covered from head to toe in red dust from riding in the back of the truck. Their hair stood up stiff with dirt and they looked like some type of cross-breed raccoon. We all laughed and breathed a sigh of relief.

We are here. I feel like I am at the edge of the earth, a beautiful place no doubt, but certainly further away from civilization as I know it, than I have ever been.

Journal Entry
January 1992

I would enjoy this experience much more if I were invisible.

I have just about had it with being continuously stared at. Our evening walks to soak in the African sunsets are often spoiled by children running along beside us, wanting to touch Bob's hairy arms, listen to us speak, and practice their own few English words. Even my home is not a place of seclusion. Children peer in our front door and open windows to watch me do housework! One day I got so irritated by the spectators that I screamed and started dancing like a mad person, thinking it would scare the children away. It didn't. I laughed at myself and then cried.

Honestly, the whole shift to living without electricity and running water has been the easy part. The physical hardship pales in comparison to the mental and spiritual challenges. The drastically different lifestyle forces me to think through everything I know: the way I was raised, the values of my home country and my own values. Why do we do the things we do? How can these people be so poor while others in the world are so wealthy? Why do these women have to work so hard and be submissive to their husbands? How can women share their husbands with several wives? The questions go on and on.

We seek common ground with our neighbors. Though our differences often outweigh our similarities, we share mutual interest in learning about each other. As I sweep my concrete floor every morning, pushing the dust out the front door, I look out at neighbors who are doing the same. We smile and greet one another. And though we struggle to communicate verbally, our eyes connect us at a much deeper level. I know that our presence here communicates our desire for friendship and outreach. Their receptive welcome reveals much more than curiosity; it shows their openness to diversity within the community.

Journal Entry
December 1992

We have finally adjusted to "African time." This term is well known by Africans and those familiar with life in Africa: it refers to a whole lifestyle – not just time on the clock. In the beginning, we chuckled about this phenomenon, in actual disbelief that it could be so different than our time-driven, task-oriented society back home. "Time is money," we had always been taught. African time refers to much more than everything and everyone being late. Yes, it incorporates many logistical realities, but it also allows for a relational element to life that somehow gets lost when societies get moving too fast.

The first wedding we attended was our real introduction to African time. We arrived at 2:45, fifteen minutes before the wedding ceremony was scheduled to begin. We were the only ones there for the following hour. Other guests began to trickle in around 4:30. The bride and photographer arrived at 4:45 and the ceremony started around 5:00. This schedule exemplifies any event, including meetings, worship services, parties and other gatherings of people.

Perhaps the only way for us to adjust to this lifestyle is to live it, not pop in and out of it at our convenience, but to be stuck smack dab in the middle of it.

Normal daily chores consume time. When you are washing every dish and piece of clothing by hand, it is often midday before you can even think about going somewhere. Then, you have to rely on public transport: one truck entering the village twice per day, overflowing with people in the back. At times these trucks are so weighted down that they can hardly maneuver the potholed roads. I hop over the tailgate of the truck, hoisting my skirt and throwing my sack to another passenger.

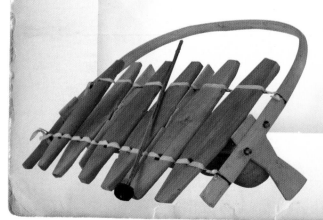

Once we stop through several villages, dropping and picking up passengers, the short distance has taken a long time. Everyone seems to understand this norm; so being late, even up to a couple of hours, is within respectable expectations. I am developing a patience that I never knew dwelled within me. Without this patience, I would either go crazy or go home.

The other day I was waiting for public transport to take me from Ibanda village to Kasese town. I shared the wait with a man who was also going to town. By the time the truck came to pick us up, an hour and a half had passed. I had so enjoyed talking with the man that I never noticed how long we had been waiting. I suddenly realized that my reference to "the people" had become "we" instead of "them." "Those people" have become my neighbors. And though I am not a native here, and will never fully understand their ways, for the moment, I am part of the community. I now understand that from a distance and even from the edge looking in, one cannot know the problems and challenges faced by people living in poverty and oppression.

Journal Entry
May 1993

Yesterday, one of our Habitat Homeowners, Donalt Ndimubanzi came to visit us at our house. As we sipped tea, he said with concern, "I hear you are leaving soon." "Oh no," I replied, "We are here through next January, at least." He asserted, "That's what I mean; January is much too soon. It would be better for you to stay at least a few more years." Besides giving us affirmation of being appreciated, Donalt's statement verified that our sense of belonging to this community is mutual.

We have spent the past few months juggling our family visitors and our everyday work here in Ibanda. It has been wonderful sharing our life here with Bob's parents, brother and friends. At the same time, their visits have been mentally challenging for me. Each visitor brings with them a piece of what is called "home." They are a physical reminder of a place, a lifestyle and people that we love dearly. It would seem that this confrontation with home would bring on "home-sickness," a longing to be back in America. However, it has not. After enjoying two weeks of vacation with Bob's parents in Kenya and Uganda, I found myself anxious to return to the village, see our dog Rwanzo and just be "home."

Bob's parents spent a week with us in Ibanda, experiencing a lifestyle that had become normal to us, but that was quite challenging for them. However, in just that short amount of time, they were able to soak in the warmth of the people who make up a community entrenched in hardships. They also experienced the love and patience of Job, as he helped them cross the river, stone by stone. All of us, including Job and especially Bob's dad John, laughed as Bob's mom Sharleen slipped on her last leap to the river's edge and soaked her entire skirt. Sharleen got the last laugh though, as John fell into the river on the return trip.

As we hiked for two hours to a church on Easter morning, Sharleen commented on having "sensory overload." In contrast, I was thinking how great it felt to be back in Ibanda. Joyful, harmonious singing filled the small mud-walled church, as people poured in with their colorful dresses and wraps. I could hear the baby behind me sucking on her mother's breast. Children looking with amazement at the white visitors filled an opened window. The preachers (there were three sermons) spoke with vigor, and though I did not understand the language, I sensed that whatever they were saying was good and powerful. I sat content, happy and spirit-filled, thinking, "It's good to be home."

The word "home" expresses many things. Bob and I often tell stories of "home" to our friends here. Home in this sense is our roots, our background and our sense of permanency.

However, home is also where your heart is. That is the kind of home we are experiencing now. Of course, we miss family and friends and the luxuries of "back home," but for now we are at peace here. We appreciate a simpler life that embraces daily human struggles and joys without the complexity of western society. We appreciate the friends we have made and the things we have learned.

Journal Entry
November 1993

For such a timeless place, time is traveling quickly these days. I guess no matter where you are, when a deadline (or term's end in our case) is approaching, numbered days are short ones. It seems just yesterday we wrote our last newsletter, yet four months have passed.

In June, Bob attended a local government meeting across the river. For his 30th birthday, I had arranged a surprise party for him. I organized friends, food, music and games. John Kumaraki, a committee member, managed to delay Bob's return from the meeting by a couple of hours.

In a culture where even church starts late, I fully expected Bob to return home and everyone else show up several hours later. I had invited our Ugandan friends weeks ahead, and had explained the importance of party guests arriving before the honored guest.

Much to my surprise, everyone arrived early, giving us a chance to practice our "SURPRISE!" a couple of times. The fact that they do not celebrate birthdays here made this preparation very important. The fact that 15 people showed up early for Bob's birthday party gave me tremendous appreciation for the friends we have made.

Job created a "Happy Birthday" banner out of newsprint flipchart paper and I hung balloons. I couldn't understand why everyone looked so embarrassed. Finally, Stephen explained that they thought I was blowing up condoms. They do not know balloons. We all had a laugh about the balloons and then took our seats, ready for Bob and John to arrive.

It worked. Bob was so surprised that he almost fell off of his bike. We celebrated cross-culturally with warm sodas, popcorn, African music on the little tape player and we ate birthday cake, topped with M&Ms I had been saving for months. It was nice to share one of our American traditions with our Ugandan friends.

Journal Entry
March 1994

I will never forget the day we left Ibanda. A range of emotions washed over me as we said our goodbyes. I felt proud of our Habitat committee members and staff who had been empowered to lead the affiliate without us. I felt relieved to have finished our term of service with a positive frame of mind. But most of all, I was overwhelmed with sadness to be leaving friends that I thought I may never see again.

They had taken us in, shared their homes and their lives with us. We had laughed at them, they had laughed at us, and eventually we were able to laugh together. We had learned from each other, and more importantly we had grown to love and respect each other, in spite of our cultural differences. I was afraid that leaving this village meant, once again, "us and them" – that the "we" was over.

Both of our hearts pounding out of our chests, Bob and I got in the pickup truck to head down the bumpy mountain road one last time. Had our dog Rwanzo not accompanied our departure, I think we would have needed to be forcefully dragged away. As we watched the village fade into the distance, we embraced each other and sobbed into each other's shoulders.

Undoubtedly, the core of my transformation occurred as a result of immersion. The experiences could have been similar but would have had different impact, had we lived on the fringes of the community. One definition of immersion is involvement in something that completely occupies all time, energy or concentration available.

The key to successful immersive living is releasing control and depending on others for survival. This submissive act is challenging for those of us who are accustomed to managing our own time and strategically planning our activities to meet goals and objectives. In order to survive in such unpredictable circumstances, Bob and I had to let go of our preconceived notions and choose to put our faith and hope in God. We accepted our vulnerable position and trusted that God was ultimately guiding our vessel. Others may choose different forms of support; however, they undeniably face similar crossroads and are pressed to question their own beliefs. Unlike living in a place of material abundance and cultural familiarity, where one can sit on the fence about her faith, immersion into a foreign culture pushes one to define what it is she's hanging on to.

I believe that God set the ultimate example of immersion when He became incarnate, through Jesus, to live among the people. Jesus' role, besides teaching God's plan, was to be a connector for us to God. It is difficult to understand God. He's too big, too out there, too mystical. We can understand Jesus much better (if we so choose) because he was a man: not a king or person of riches and status, but a common man who related to all people, especially the poor.

I also believe that the best leaders for the community, the churches and the governments are those who have lived at the grassroots level of the population they are serving. Through the years, we have seen many failed development efforts, intended to trickle down to the people. Having lived with some of the poorest people, I can tell you that most aid gets clogged somewhere at the top before it has a chance to trickle down. When the decision makers have a true understanding of poverty issues, community development has a better chance of succeeding.

Perhaps the process of returning to our home culture was more difficult after such an intense immersive living experience. However, the gained insights and spiritual rewards made it worthwhile. The temporary loss of identity experienced upon return to the states was all part of the transformative process that would continue our thirst for "living on faith." As John Ortburg states in his book, *If You Want to Walk on Water, You've got to Get Out of the Boat*, "walking on water means facing your fears and choosing not to let fear have the last word." Ortburg's book is about acting on faith, stepping in with both feet and trusting that you will not sink. I interpret his writing to mean immersion into real Christian living. Immersion, in any sense, encompasses letting go of fears, trusting others and keeping focused on a purpose.

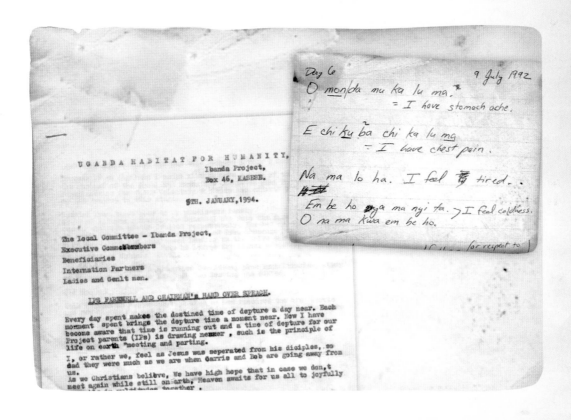

Simple, Decent and Affordable

We should live simply, yet not prohibiting quality and pleasure. Use of technology must be appropriate: for our locale and its natural resources, our children and the health of our family, and ultimately, the sustainability of life. If we keep our spending within our means, we can enjoy a lifestyle that embraces fulfilling work and meaningful relationships.

We just fell in love with the mission of Habitat for Humanity. As volunteers on a Habitat work team with our church in Charlotte, we had experienced the fun and fulfillment that comes from slinging a hammer with a Habitat homeowner. As a newly married couple and just a few years out of college, we were much more comfortable showing God's love than speaking about it. So after months of research on international service organizations, both Christian and secular, we knew that Habitat was a perfect fit for our desire to put "faith in action."

Putting faith in action was only one piece of the Habitat puzzle that excited us. Habitat's foundational principles encompass so many of the values that Bob and I share, not only through our Christian upbringing, but also from our convictions about human rights and social justice.

The best summary of Habitat's principles is stated in Habitat's Mission Focus.

Mission Focus

1) Demonstrate the love and teachings of Jesus Christ.
2) Provide a way of sharing between the affluent and those in need.
3) Work in partnership with representative local leadership.
4) Select families in greatest need first, without favoritism or discrimination.
5) Construct simple, decent and affordable houses together.
6) Sell houses at no profit, with no interest added and use payments to build more houses.

Of course, simple, decent and affordable are relative terms, only definable at the local level. In fact, choosing an appropriate house design is one of the tasks required of every Habitat affiliate around the world. In various nations, states, counties and cities, Habitat committees design homes that are 1) simple in structure, yet meet basic human needs for adequate space and healthy shelter 2) decent in terms of quality of construction, durability and local building codes and 3) affordable, such that the cost of the home can be repaid by low income wage earners within a reasonable period of time. From coastal wood houses built on stilts to well-insulated adobe houses, Habitat's use of appropriate building technology varies greatly worldwide. Simple, decent and affordable – what a great principle.

July 1992
Dear John and Sharleen,

Greetings from the beautiful Rwenzori Mountains of the Moon! From our back garden we can see snow-capped peaks on clear days. And yes, we are barely 15 kilometers from the equator. Can you imagine? The elevation brings temperate climate, much more desirable than the hot nights in Kasese town, just a few kilometers down the dusty mountain road. We are happy here.

There is an aspect of our work that you would find particularly interesting. In building Habitat houses, we strive to use appropriate technology in order to keep the houses simple, decent and affordable. In rural Uganda, that means building with materials that can be gathered on site, using lots of unskilled labor and combining traditional building techniques with new ones that offer more long-term durability.

In Ibanda, the clay soil is quite good for brick making. Job Malighee is pioneering a brick making industry on his land. He has constructed wooden molds to be used for shaping the wet clay. Once the clay has been mashed into a mold, the wet brick is laid out to sun dry. After 300-500 bricks have been formed, they are stacked together in the shape of a kiln, leaving a hollowed out place for a fire. Then, Job packs mud around the bricks to form an outer protective wall of the kiln.

Long timbers are placed in the hull of the kiln and set on fire. After the fire has burned for several days and the coals have cooled down, the outer coating of hardened mud is removed. The fired bricks are now ready for building.

Fired bricks are certainly an upgrade from the traditional mud walls of the houses in Ibanda. However, when constructed carefully, mud walls with an external plaster of cow dung can be quite durable. Many of our Habitat homeowners cannot afford a brick house, even if they make their own bricks. We have a special loan for roofs and floors only. This program addresses the main problems with the traditional housing. Dirt floors breed disease and poorly thatched grass roofs leak and harbor insect nesting.

In International Partner training we spent a full month learning various building techniques for developing countries. At the beginning of this learning curve, I was astonished that houses could be built for under 1,000 US dollars. Now that we have a better understanding of the socio-economic situation in rural Africa, we are working with our Habitat committee to continually cut house costs even more in order to make Habitat houses within financial reach of the average farmer here.

A few months ago, Bob and I asked our committee to show us the best local building techniques. They suggested that we visit the home of Stephen Baluku. We already knew two of Stephen's brothers: Nyasyo is a carpenter who builds door and window frames for the Habitat houses, and his teen brother Tom occasionally does yard work for us. Stephen's house is just up the mountain from ours. It would be a day's outing – because any outing somehow swallows the day.

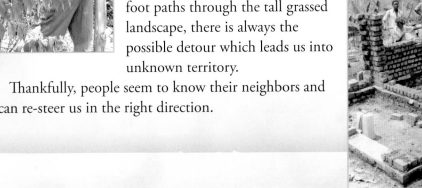

The walks here are very pleasurable for us. The surroundings are beautiful, in a natural and unkempt kind of way. It is a heavily farmed area, but the crops are planted and harvested among steep hillsides that lead to a backdrop of majestic, mysterious mountains. Every hike offers some type of adventure. The adventure can be as simple as a cultural blunder that sends everyone into hysteria, or it can be as challenging as crossing a gushing river by jumping stone to stone. And while we have come to know the many foot paths through the tall grassed landscape, there is always the possible detour which leads us into unknown territory.

Thankfully, people seem to know their neighbors and can re-steer us in the right direction.

I find this amazing, as the average farmer has three to four acres of land. With tall growing crops such as banana and coffee trees, I find it easy to get lost on just one man's plot of land.

As we were preparing for our day's outing, Job came to our door and greeted us as usual, "*Wabukiri. Waheno?*" (Good morning. How is here?) I offered Job a seat and a cup of tea as he would wait for us to finish preparing ourselves for the day.

Job continued talking to us as we went about our business, "I am ready to take you to Stephen's. Bob, I can smell your good soap. Is it from America?"

Bob answered from the bedroom where he was washing his face in a little plastic basin, "Yes Job, it came in a care package."

"Ahhhh, you have such nice things in your country," Job replied.

Bob was embarrassed that such a simple thing as soap was yet another symbol of the luxuries that we take for granted.

Job always wears a warm smile and is ready to give his time and full attention. He has become our host, teaching us the language and guiding us through physical and cultural barriers. It is not a formal relationship – it just somehow came to be. Job turns up every morning ready to accompany us through the day.

Job finished his tea just as we finished preparing the house for departure. We always close the window shutters in case we get an unexpected downpour or a gust of wind that blows a red blanket of dust into our home.

When we are at home, all of our windows and our two doors remain open. This means that we are in and anyone is welcome to visit. And they do. We have visitors every day. Yesterday, we had an unwelcome visitor – a chicken wandered in, and left us a little present on the floor – and it wasn't an egg. One of the benefits of having a smooth concrete floor is that things wipe up easily.

Windows shut, doors locked, water bottles filled, sunscreen applied, and hats plopped on our heads, we set out for our journey to Stephen Baluku's house.

As we approached Stephen's house, we called out, "*Tunako?*" (Anybody home?) "*Ehhh, Tunayo,*" (You are welcome) Stephen said in his quiet, sincere voice. I sensed a humble manner about him from the moment I met him.

Stephen is a strong and somewhat rugged man, but he speaks softly and gently, using only the few words needed to communicate beyond his actions. He is well known for his craftsmanship in building.

Stephen's house has the charm of a little cottage in the woods. With a well-crafted grass thatched roof, the house has exterior mud walls plastered with cow dung. These walls are painted in a pastel yellow, complemented by decorative orange flowers painted under the window sills. The dirt path that meanders through the garden up to the house is clean and bordered with indigenous shrubs that have little yellow flowers.

We dropped our shoes by the front door and entered into this little house that is just as neat and clean on the inside as it is on the outside. Stephen offered us seats in their sitting room and his wife quickly came to greet us by kneeling in front of us and slightly bowing her head, "*Wasubiri.*" (Good afternoon) Women generally kneel to men. They sometimes kneel to me as well; I guess the fact that I am a white woman confuses the normal status structure.

After sharing tea and biscuits Stephen's wife served, we set out on our "appropriate technology" tour. Stephen explained every step of the building process. He took us to the river and showed us where he gets the reeds for building the structural wall frames. As we walked through his land, he whacked a variety of grasses with his *panga* (big knife). Stephen took a sample of many natural resources: flowers, berries, sandy soil, clay, and rocks, and then showed us where they had been used in the building process. He seemed to have found a use for everything on his land.

The highlight of the tour for me was when he made paint. He had already demonstrated making a paint brush out of grass and banana fibers. He had also gathered the ingredients for the paint: a light colored soil with just enough water mixed in to make it pasty, and some yellow flowers for the pigment.

Stephen began kneading the mud, using his hands to mix in the ground up flowers, and then gently looked up and said, "Oh, I almost forgot…"
He walked into the dirt road and with his hand scooped up a big pile of cow poop and plopped it into the mixture.

I don't think Stephen actually saw our facial expressions but somehow he sensed that this procedure might be out of our comfort zone. He then gave us a grin of wisdom that I'll remember for my lifetime and said, "Don't mind this; it's my business."

Working the mud paste and cow dung together, adding enough water to achieve the correct viscosity, Stephen made a creamy yellow paint that would be a best seller for interior designers back home.

As I looked at the meticulously designed, constructed and decorated house, built solely out of the resources on Stephen's land, I thought, "Now, that is Simple, Decent and very Affordable."

Much Love,
Carrie

"Simple, decent and affordable" has become a standard of measure for many aspects of my life today. Certainly, our house is our family's biggest personal expense as well as our most valuable asset. So building and buying within our means is of utmost importance. Additionally, living within our means should describe our other consumer practices. When purchasing clothes, food, cars, electronic equipment, etc., I make a practice of asking, "Is it simple, decent and affordable?" (For us)

Well, that sounds just boring, you may think. On the contrary, using this type of practical thinking allows us to engage in fulfilling work (which for us is within the non-profit sector) and stretch our means (the non-profit salary) to enjoy many of life's pleasures. When "simple, decent and affordable" is our standard practice, we are able to enjoy the occasional splurge: the adventurous vacation, a new camera, a piece of art, a fine ceramic, or a handmade craft.

Do Bob and I live within our means? Not fully. We have debt on an equity line for roofing and painting our house and other major home repairs. We take nice vacations and dream of others that we cannot afford. Our thirst for experiencing different cultures and seeing new places is part of our family's life. Though we cannot afford to travel every year, we continually seek ways to save for occasional adventures. We are cognizant of a simple life and strive to achieve balance between wants and needs.

Appropriate use of technology plays a significant role in our consumer decision-making process as well. People generally associate the term appropriate technology with agriculture, industry and use of natural resources. I have utmost respect for the organizations and individuals who are exploring and pushing technologies that are appropriate for the longevity of the earth, people's lives and the sustainability of all for future generations. My sphere of influence, at the moment, is my children. It is imperative that Bob and I, as parents, choose appropriate use of technology for our family. I struggle with the modern trend of excessive use of electronics. In my opinion, children and young adults are spending too much time in a set of earphones, watching a screen of some sort and playing electronic games that allow them to tune out everything while entering a world of virtual relationships and adventures.

The seductive nature of electronic devices threatens a quality of life that we have always enjoyed – playing board games, exploring new hikes, reading, and telling stories around the fire like we used to do in Africa. I am determined to guard our family from the excessive screen time that has become the norm in our American culture.

Of course we use cell phones, computers and digital cameras for personal and professional needs. However, all technology is not appropriate for me or my children. We evaluate every purchase on the scale of appropriateness. Just because "everybody has one" is not a good enough assessment or reason to make it appropriate for us. We strive to balance technology in our home with our value of relational living and continue to ask, "Is this technology appropriate for us in our attempt to maintain a simple, decent and affordable life?"

Trash and Treasure

One man's trash is another man's treasure, especially in places where there is little trash: places where everything is used for something. People with limited resources learn how to make the most of what they have by recycling, re-using, or re-engineering to serve another purpose. Ultimately, there should be no such thing as trash.

We had barely finished writing thank you notes for all of our wedding presents when my beloved husband announced that he had quit his job. "I'm not feeling that this is where I'm supposed to be or that I'm doing the type of work I'm supposed to be doing." With a business degree from Wake Forest University, Bob was moving along successfully in computer sales; however, he was no longer fulfilled or challenged in his work.

I learned early in our marriage that I had married a man who would follow his dreams, stepping out on faith and swimming through muddy waters to get to where he felt he was needed. His sense of adventure and yearning for purposeful living were in fact some of the qualities that drew me into his crystal blue eyes. And when we said our wedding vows, we promised to support each other to "grow into all that God had intended." Though I wasn't thrilled that I would become the bread winner while he researched a good fit for our desire to serve overseas, I still cherished the man I married and admired his courage to step into the unknown.

My job in print sales floated us financially, and it was only another six months before we were packing up all of those wedding presents and putting them safely in storage so that we could head down to Habitat for Humanity for International Partner Training. The process of downsizing our possessions to fit into two suitcases was somehow cleansing and refreshing. Where were we going to put all that stuff anyway?

Do not store up for yourselves treasures on earth, where moth and rust destroy, and where thieves break in and steal. But store up for yourselves treasures in heaven, where moth and rust do not destroy, and where thieves do not break in and steal. For where your treasure is, there your heart will be also.

Matthew: 6: 19-21

April 1992
Dear Rich,

Our move from Kasese to the village of Ibanda has been an answer to prayer.
I sense that this community has the potential to develop a truly grassroots house
building program. One thing is for sure – there are tremendous needs here. In fact,
housing is but one of the horrible living conditions. This area lacks potable water,
medical facilities and adequate schools. Poverty is standard.

Nearly a year now into our term, I realize that I have adjusted my lifestyle
and personal habits beyond my wildest imagination. The trips to the latrine in
the darkest of night, using only a flashlight that flickers on and off at its own
will, has become a normal routine. Squatting over a little hole in the ground is
so commonplace that the treks out into the darkness barely interrupt my vivid
dreams.

Our pared down wardrobe has proven adequate for village life, where we
alternate between two outfits a week, merely shaking off the copper-hued dust and
hanging them to air dry from the day's sweat. Knowing the dirt promised by each
day makes it hardly worth putting on freshly washed clothes; but more than that,
the labor and use of scarce water required for laundering prohibits more than a
once-a-week washing. And, flipping our underwear inside-out allows us to extend
their wear as well. The lack of clothing choice is not an issue for us, although
I occasionally long to put on a pair of jeans. Wearing trousers is culturally
inappropriate for women, as is showing any leg above the knees. I often think,
"When I get done here, I'll never put on a jumper-style, ankle-length dress again."

Cooking with five staple ingredients began as a challenge but has become a
source of pride as I creatively cook a variety of meals using only tomatoes, potatoes,
onions, rice and carrots. With three cooking pots, six plastic plates and bowls, and
a single kerosene burner stove, I put many dinners on the table. Not gourmet – not
even tasty at times, but certainly acceptable and practical.

Though it has taken me a long time to stomach purchasing meat at the open
market, I have mastered that art as well, knowing which "cuts" to ask for and

how to tell if it has "slept a night." This means that it was slaughtered the day before. With no refrigeration, it is extremely important to buy and cook meat on slaughter day and plan for just the amount that can be eaten within the day.

The challenge of course, is anticipating whether we will receive drop-in visitors for dinner. Though we can always extend the table, it is embarrassing to have a puny meal cooked for two, as we are most likely the only couple in the village without children to feed. Since we have no way of keeping leftovers from spoiling, I cook "just enough"– for two, that is. I think that our neighbors have learned how peculiar American's meal customs are – that visitors are welcome when they have been invited and planned for, but that having spontaneous guests for dinner is beyond stressful. Thankfully, we have melded into their custom of serving tea and biscuits to drop-in visitors, and they pardon us for our inability to stretch dinner on a regular basis. The cross-cultural understanding brings comfort to our friendships, which enables us to enjoy shared meals. Our Ugandan friends feel like honored guests when they have been invited to join us for the evening. And I have come to expect and enjoy the daily drop-in visitors for tea time.

Another lifestyle habit we have developed is living on 20-30 gallons of water per week, every drop carried to our kitchen from the village water tap, which is around 100 meters from our house. Twice or thrice a week, Bob goes to the water tap with two five- gallon jerry cans to collect our water. Jerry cans, commonly used throughout Africa, are yellow plastic jugs used to haul liquids. In the beginning, it was embarrassing that this was a man's role in our family, since he was the only man at the water tap with all the village women and children. But we have resolved that it is not worth encumbering my 95-pound body by carrying ten gallons of water to "fit in" to cultural norms. Bob's role as water carrier is not culturally offensive; rather it's a mzungu oddity.

An example of offensive cultural habits is any public display of affection between spouses. Bob and I have given up the idea of walking on the road holding hands because the spectacle created by our action strips away the joy and comfort that the affection provides. We do however, still sit together during meals, and I think that our admiration for each other is visible in other ways. Sometimes, our committee members' smirks of embarrassment convey their discomfort with our attraction to each other. They tell us that public affection of any degree between spouses indicates too much interest in sex.

From the 20 gallons of water, ten is boiled and kept in a jug with a pour spout for drinking, while the rest is used for cooking and cleaning. Only recently, when we had some visitors from America, did we recognize that our drinking water, which is boiled and stored in a five-gallon camping container, is a yellowish-brown. We know that all parasites are killed from boiling the water, so we consider it "clean." Our water bottles have stained from their treacherous journeys up and down the Rwenzori Mountains, and our white tee shirts have all become shades of tan. So, "clears" and "whites" have faded from our expectations and murky drinking water has become our norm.

Bob and I have become skilled at bathing (including our hair) with a small bowl of water, using a plastic mug to scoop and trickle the water from strategic starting points on our bodies. The conservation of water has pushed me to cut my hair very short, a style I haven't worn since grade school. Only once did I cry about it being cut so short that I looked like a man. We do our splash baths in the corner of our bedroom, which has a drain hole in the sloped cement floor. Unlike our neighbors who simply bathe by the moonlight, we prefer a little privacy, since our white bodies reflect every moonbeam rather than blending into the night's darkness.

On all fronts, I have learned to live simply and with minimal "things." There is not an unused item in the house. Still, in comparison to my neighbors, I have stuff galore. We have pictures of family on the walls of our 300-square-foot brick house. Our house is of a size and quality that villagers aspire to attain. We have a small tape player with two fist sized speakers. And of course, we have a steady supply of AA batteries to run this sophisticated stereo. Our care packages from home (thank you!) and our trips to the capital city keep us stocked with amenities unavailable in our village. We have books, photo albums, camera equipment and medicine – all luxury items that our neighbors do not have.

And we have trash, a huge curiosity to our neighbors, especially the children. By American standards, our trash is minimal; but still, what do you do with trash in a place where there is no trash collection or community dump? Well, of course, you burn it. We dug our own fire pit in our backyard and much less frequently than we wash clothes, we burn a pile of trash, the things that will not decompose in our compost pile.

An image that will impress upon me for life occurred after one of our trash burnings. A child was running around the village pulling a twine string with his new toy attached. He had constructed a well-crafted sports car out of the Corn Flakes box that I had pitched in our fire pit.

We certainly did not notice the box missing during our burning, nor had we seen any trash scavengers scouting out our pile. It is noteworthy that Corn Flakes are a luxury to us. Only an occasional trip to the capital city of Kampala brings such boxed and canned commodities that are so craved and treasured, even if served with warm, boxed, ultra-pasteurized milk.

How did we miss the potential value of the box with the rooster on the front? At first, I was amused and impressed by the child's creativity. On second thought, I was ashamed for throwing away a box that obviously had a second life. I was also reminded of all the waste and trash in my home country: the landfills; the half-eaten over-packaged snacks that topple over public trash cans surrounded by bees; the cereal boxes, other food product containers and cleaning solution bottles that fill the grocery store shelves; the excessive "stuff" that fills American homes and often becomes the very clutter that consumes productive time and energy.

Once again, the imbalance of resources and opportunities on the global scale of human consumption create overwhelming sadness for me.

I know that you are witnessing many of the same discrepancies in India. I pray that you are well and that God is protecting you in your overseas endeavor.

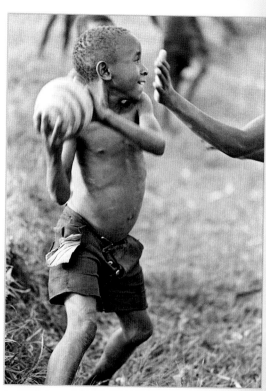

Love,
Carrie

Trash and Treasure. I sometimes obsess over eating every last bit of food on the table or putting out leftovers over and over. My dress is often a 1980s fashion statement. Though I appreciate nice clothes, new fashions, and as most American women wish for, a wardrobe that enhances my figure, my true value of distinguishing wants from needs defines the way I spend money on clothes and other commodities.

Seeking eco-friendly cleaning products and re-using every container until it falls apart are both integral to my housekeeping practices. I have a hard time throwing anything away. Though I clean out our "stuff" quarterly, selling and giving to places that can use the things we have outgrown, I never cease to feel the invasion of clutter that finds its way into our home.

The buildup of stuff often sends me over the edge, as I go into a rampage with my kids over how spoiled we Americans are. The best example of this is the Christmas day that I packed up all the kids' gifts in a sack and took them back! They had demonstrated less appreciation than I thought they should have shown and had even gotten a little whiny midday. I thought of all the kids who receive the shoebox of gifts that we send through Samaritan's Purse and imagined how thrilled they must be to get a toothbrush, a pair of socks, and a bouncy ball. I think my kid's "got it" after many tears and accusations of me being the "meanest mom in the world." I gave back their presents the following day. And life went on with a new meaning and appreciation for Christmas.

Hopefully, the aversion to wastefulness will help our family distinguish wants from needs and keep us prudent in our choices, allowing intentional saving, spending and giving. This is a practice that has to be continually kept in check, as we are exposed to an array of seductively advertised merchandise. We do have nice things, we do have a nice house, we do have more than we need; but we also have a global perspective which keeps us cognizant of seeking the balance between trash and treasures.

My Life of Luxury

Anything beyond meeting basic needs is luxury. Anything beyond "just enough" can become consuming, excessive and burdensome. Luxury is maintaining a life of "just enough" – that place in between "too little" and "too much."

Never before had I considered myself wealthy. I certainly knew by the time I was in middle school that I lived a privileged life. Being part of a white middle-class American family offered opportunities unseen to other classes, races and nationalities.

My parents raised four children (I am the youngest) with Christian values, emphasizing the golden rule, a compassionate worldview, frugality and gratitude. Though I was at times jealous of the amount of stuff my friends got for Christmas, my most remembered and cherished Christmas was the time our family worked at the homeless shelter on Christmas eve and woke up to my dad saying, "Pack a suitcase, we're heading to the NC mountains to go snow skiing." My parents demonstrated the essence of Jesus' birth by giving us an opportunity to be among the poor and disheartened, yet then surprising us with a day of family fun on the slopes.

I knew what it meant to work for my money. My first job at 11 years old was rubber-banding and delivering 150 newspapers twice a week for $3.00 pay. While the pay was hardly worth the effort, it did afford an occasional movie. But more importantly, the job set a precedent for a life that would embrace a good work ethic. Since that time, I have had many jobs, some self-created, others undesirable, but all producing an earned buck.

The point is that I went to Africa thinking I was neither wealthy nor spoiled, and came back knowing that I am both. Unlike some of the memories that have faded over time, this realization has penetrated my self-awareness to the extent that it is part of my daily mantra, "I am wealthy, I am blessed, and I am thankful."

November 1991
Dear Mom and Dad,

The alarm rings at 4:45 am, which is quite a bit earlier than our usual awakening by the rooster crow at 6:30 am. I reach my arm out of the mosquito net that drapes our bed, to find the nearest candle and matches. The air is still, but not as hot as it had been last night when we were trying to fall asleep. Knowing we would leave early and in darkness, we had only to brush our teeth and make a last latrine stop before taking a moonlit walk to Kasese town. Our village is quiet. We hear only the sound of our feet scuffling along the dusty road. We carry our luggage, which consists of a duffle bag, a camera and a water bottle. The bus to Kampala leaves at 6 am from the post office in town. We board the bus and pray for safe travel. Bob spots a Habitat committee member and sits with him in order to talk business on the road. I take the seat just behind them.

As people begin to fill up the bus, I observe them, wondering what their purpose of travel is, for it is only a small percentage of Ugandans that get an opportunity to leave their village and journey to the capital city. Is it business? Do they have family in Kampala? Are they seeking work? Are they bringing back commodities to sell?

A woman dressed in a traditional *basuti* (dress) boards the bus, carrying lots of luggage and her baby tied on her back. I know that she has on her very best dress for the trip. Her head is wrapped in a green cloth imprinted with red roosters. She comes to sit beside me, the skinny white woman with additional space in my seat. She first unties the knot at her chest and then the knot at her waist, both securing the fabric sling that holds her baby on her back. I look up at her and give an assuring smile that I will hold her baby as she sorts out her many bags and gets them to the back of the bus. "*Wabukiri Mama,*" I say, assuming she is from the Bakonzo tribe. "*Ehhh, Wabukiri,*" she responds, with an even bigger smile. I am relieved that I have greeted her in her language and not the language of the tribe that has oppressed her people for generations.

As I hold this beautiful baby, all wrapped and diapered for the trip, I am glad she has a cloth on her bottom. I never know what happens to all the excretions of the naked babies. I also think of the strain it must be for a woman to travel alone with a child. Where is she going and why is she leaving? Why does she have what is probably all of her possessions with her? Typically when women travel with children, they are going back to their home village because they have either left their husband or been thrown out.

The mother comes back and sits down beside me, taking her baby back to her own arms. It's only seconds before the baby is happily nursing. We exchange smiles, knowing it is the only communication we are capable of sharing with each other, for I have exhausted my extent of surface level greetings in Lukonzo. It would be a non-talkative trip, though contemplative as we sat curious about each other's lives. I'm sure she was wondering what in the heck I was doing there and what my life is like and why I don't have a baby at my back.

In the darkness, the bus ride is like an amusement park rollercoaster. The bus travels fast over bumpy and curvy roads. I close my eyes and escape to another place, praying all the while that the bus will not dip into one of the many potholes and turn upside down. When I begin long journeys, I think of the public transport accident that Bob had a few months ago. When his driver lost control, the matatu veered off the road and several passengers suffered mild injuries. The one child on board was quickly picked up by another passing vehicle and was rushed to a hospital. The remaining passengers, including Bob, waited for hours on the side of the road for assistance, even though some of them needed medical care. The trauma for me was that I did not know what had happened until someone came to my door delivering the message that Bob had been in an accident and was at Kilembe Hospital. Without phones, communication is slow and unreliable. I reached the hospital and found Bob resting – the deep gash in his elbow had been stitched up. Bob's accident reminds me to count our blessings and to pray for protection on all journeys.

As the sun rises, we are traveling through Queen Elizabeth National Park.

The beauty and serenity of the African plains greets me: the tall wispy grass, the candelabra trees, the acacia trees with their flat, stretched-out tops, and of course the wildlife. I feel like I'm in a movie as we pass baboons and watch Ugandan kob bounce across the road. We also go through the midlands, which hosts miles of banana forests and tea plantations. The eight- hour bus ride to Kampala, though tiresome, is an exhilarating microcosm of life in rural Africa. I have to trust the driver and fellow travelers, and ultimately that God will get me there safely. While my faith is stretched, I absorb and appreciate the unique character of Africa – simply graceful, unbelievably beautiful, yet ruggedly harsh, all at the same time.

We stop in small towns to allow other travelers to board. Though there is not always time to get out and find a restroom (or more truthfully, a bush to squat behind) there are always snacks for purchase. Many "hawkers" push their foods and goods through the bus windows, exchanging money as they go. The variety includes goat meat on a stick, boiled eggs, samosas (meat pies), roasted corn, chapatis (South Asian flat bread), and warm bottled sodas. I quite enjoy the samosas. The Indian food influence is still prevalent, as Indians had a large presence in the business economy before Idi Amin threw them out of the country. The Ugandan food selection is a blend of cultures.

We reach Kampala at 2:30 pm and take another, smaller, public bus to the center of town, called Taxi Park. Now, here is a place of chaos! Hundreds of white matatus, all packed into a huge lot, park momentarily to load and offload passengers. The vehicles come and go, squeezing by each other with less than a couple of inches between. The minivans dodge pedestrians, although it is the pedestrian's responsibility to not get hit. Taxi Park is the hub for matatus going everywhere in the city and to all major towns in the country. There are no signs or indications as to where the vehicles are going. You just have to ask and weave your way through the maze to find the right vehicle.

Even finding our way out of Taxi Park is challenging. I always look for the trash pile invaded by Maribu storks; this is the landmark for the part of the city that we are trying to reach. A first-time experience here is hair-raising for all visitors. Bob and I have gotten used to the chaos, and though not completely at ease, we know how to find our way.

We make our way out of the matatu maze to the streets of Kampala. The city is bustling with street vendors, selling practically everything, including underwear, jewelry, batteries, music tapes – you name it. People are moving in every direction, marketing their goods with hope of making their day's wage. I sometimes think that I could get all of my shopping done and not step foot into a store.

Besides the bustle of people, the sidewalks are filled with potholes, broken cement slabs and uncovered manholes. The atrocities of Idi Amin's rule are evident in the broken windows of buildings and hanging telephone wires. Signs of a war-torn city prevail, though a hopeful spirit permeates the process of repair and new construction. While I am encouraged to see lots of construction – digging, laying blocks, mixing cement, placing pipes and wires – the rebuilding process makes for an obstacle course for pedestrians. The dichotomy is overwhelming and I am reminded that I am a "glass half full" girl. Gotta hang on to that. I watch every step with awareness that professional bag-slitters lurk, threatening to "pick" just about anything I have without my knowledge. It is not a peaceful stroll through the city.

Our first destination is always the post office, where we can send a fax home and occasionally make a phone call. There is a wait (sometimes an hour), and even still, the calls do not always go through, making for another trip to the post office the following day. The rest of our time in the city is spent shopping for staple supplies and meeting with our in-country Habitat staff.

We all bring our project problems to discuss, and enjoy amenities like restaurants and ice-cream shops.

We can even catch a little bit of news on CNN International at the Sheraton lobby. Of course, news is always bad, so just as well to be uninformed since there is nothing we can do to change anything. In fact, we are always shocked at how little we know about what is going on outside of our rural village. We have become "villagers" and like other members of our community, we long to go home from the city – back to the big starry sky and security of known neighbors.

Our quarterly trips to Kampala are simply to take care of business. They are a craved escape and a wearisome reminder that rural life is not so bad. We come home by way of another eight hour bus ride, carrying baskets of commodities like peanut butter, pasta and canned tuna, to be rationed over months. Always happy to return to our little home with a view, our own bed with a mosquito net, and the sounds of frogs and crickets perched outside of our open windows.

Missing You, Carrie

They're all relative: wealth, poverty, luxuries and hardships. There is always someone more healthy, wealthy and wise than you. And, there are also those who have less, suffer more, or struggle to meet their daily needs. There is wealth and poverty in most countries; however, the breadth of that spectrum within each country varies greatly. The differences in wealth, consumption of resources and poverty between first world and third world countries are mind boggling.

Though my awareness of these discrepancies occasionally produces pangs of guilt, (in fact I have struggled through several depressions based on this awareness) I have come to understand that guilt-rendered action and giving solely from a position of abundance are not sacredly revered. Rather, with appreciation for my blessings, I am to live responsibly, serving others and giving out of my gratitude. The transformation from guilt to gratitude has cemented for me only within the past two years. That transformation, sifted through God's grace, has set me free from the grip of depression.

Honestly, I have never felt comfortable saying that I am "blessed" because I live in middle class America. Why should I have received that blessing, and not someone else? I have read countless books on poverty and third world countries written by anthropologists, historians, economists, theologians and other scholars. For me, the arguments and analysis of why the world is the way it is do not reconcile the gap between the haves and the have-nots. And though from an intellectual standpoint, I understand development theories, supply and demand, political structures and cultural conflicts, my heart breaks over and over at the realities. Thus, I practice over and over putting my "fix it" personality into neutral gear and focusing on what I have some influence over. This, of course, simply includes my attitude, the way I spend my time, the way I raise my children and the way I nurture the many personal relationships that I have been blessed with.

I often think back to events like the bus ride to Kampala and compare those days to my current day-to-day activities. It is these comparisons that exaggerate my life of luxury. So many "normal" conveniences in this country are taken for granted. Our normal day includes numerous activities that are a struggle for rural Africans.

Luxury is waking up in a house with a solid roof that has kept the rain and the varmints out, having slept in a comfortable bed with the security of a peaceful neighborhood.

Luxury is doing laundry in an automatic washing machine. Even though I sometimes complain about the amount of dirty clothes my kids produce, I am ever thankful for my Kenmore® washer.

Luxury is owning a car and driving wherever and whenever I need to go. The rising gas prices seem to make us negligent of appreciating this luxury. My awfully worn, ten year-old Toyota van, as un-cool as it is to my kids, is an absolute luxury. I can haul extra people, our bikes and camping gear. We take long road trips very comfortably, stopping at many clean restrooms and restaurants. At home, we make all of our stops around town with ease and timeliness.

Luxury is being able to exercise for fitness and good health. I have just run my first half marathon. During training, every run is an opportunity to convene with God and my beautiful natural surroundings (and to think about this book's next chapter).

Luxury is having choices about what to eat and being able to establish healthy eating habits.

Luxury is choosing a field of study and a life of work based on my interests, talents and gifts. It is having free public schools and having opportunities for higher education accessible to a broad socio-economic class. Again, luxury is freedom of choice.

Luxury is taking a vacation. It is being able to take a break from the fast-paced American life, an opportunity to enjoy family, refocus on priorities, and rest our bodies and minds.

Luxury is having the choice to live simply and acquire "just enough" to live comfortably and efficiently. Unfortunately, this freedom of choice often succumbs to the temptations that "more is better" and we fall into the trap of excessive consumerism. Then, the luxury of choice becomes a burden as we struggle to pay for, maintain and replace our material goods.

Luxury is having quality healthcare that is available and affordable. While affordable insurance is unattainable for a large percentage of Americans, many of us benefit from childhood vaccines and doctor visits when we are ill.

The biggest and most taken-for-granted luxury is having water: clean water to drink, water that flows through a tap into your home, hot water to shower and enough water to clean your clothes. I started to write a chapter simply on water, but the truth is that there are not enough words to describe the lack of this essential resource for life.

What I have just described as luxuries encompasses the American dream. When these luxuries are obtained, families have the potential to live a simple and fulfilling life and much more; they can look to achieving personal and community goals. Basic needs are met. Modern technology makes for efficient use of time and minimal duplicated effort. Yet, these luxuries, which are certainly not achieved by everyone in American society, but for those who enjoy them – are often taken for granted. The luxury of "just enough" weakens to the magnet of "more" and this imbalance often impoverishes individuals, families and communities. The excessive nature of American culture affects the global economy and balance of natural resources, leaving developing nations in even more dire straits.

My current challenge is raising children to be responsible adults within a country of abundance. The societal lure of "more, bigger, better, and faster" competes for our children's attention. "Just enough" doesn't attract their desires. While my African counterparts struggle to provide decent housing, food, and education for their children, we struggle with all the choices for education, sports and other extra-curricular activities. Our basic needs are met and we are inundated with new technologies that continue to make our days busier, more hurried and less relational.

Seeing "more, more, more" promotes "I want, I want, I want." The cycle of poverty mirrors the cycle of materialism.

Both revolve simultaneously, with little awareness of the other. As a parent, I feel responsible for raising children to know God's love and grace for them, and to appreciate cultural and socio-economic diversity. Understanding that the burdens of the imbalanced world are too heavy for children, we try to inject "just enough" global awareness into our family life to promote appreciation without spoiling the fun. Having fun and enjoying simple pleasures are among our top values as well.

While preparing our children to be adults who are highly functional in a global work force is certainly one of our goals, more true to the cause is our hope that they will appreciate their lives of luxury and live responsibly out of their gratitude.

My Life of Job

Inevitably we will trudge through valleys and long dark tunnels, suffering physically, emotionally and spiritually. We may lose control of everything except for, possibly, our own attitudes. If we take the time to be still, listening for and seeking direction, we will find a crack through which a gleam of light peaks through. And if we follow the light, having faith that it will bring us out of darkness, we have the opportunity to experience the greatness of life tenfold: the chance to see things we've never seen, do things we've always been afraid of and appreciate life for all it is intended to be.

I write this chapter out of a sense of responsibility, not desire. I will take you into my places of darkness; I will share my spiritual doubts, my bouts with depression and my loss of hope in the goodness of mankind.

How audacious of me to claim "My Life of Job." My physical hardships do not compare to those of the "Jobs," nor does my faith measure up to theirs. The only parallel I can draw is the steadfastness of God's grace, power and love – no matter the Job, no matter the circumstances.

I do not believe that sheer suffering teaches. If suffering alone taught, all the world would be wise, since everyone suffers. To suffering must be added mourning, understanding, patience, love, openness and the willingness to remain vulnerable.

Anne Morrow Lindbergh,
American writer and poet

October 1991

Dear John and Sharleen,

We just wanted to contribute our little bit to make the world a better place. We wanted to share God's love with others through our work. We wanted to share our blessings and experience our faith in an active way, yet our hopes and dreams are being challenged as we sink deeper into the work.

Although our arrival in Africa and first few months were exciting and fulfilling, the honeymoon is over. We have settled in here, and so have the realities. I am frustrated. All committee members are expecting houses. Rwenzori Habitat covers an extensive area in a mountainous region where remote villages lie beyond our reach. We have no vehicle. Committee members travel from these remote places and turn up at our doorstep and ask why we haven't started building houses for them. Legal land titles are neither obtainable nor affordable for the common person. Mortgages are a foreign concept for subsistent farmers, yet they are required in Habitat's program. The Habitat house plans are too big and too expensive for the people in need of decent shelter. These are just a few of the problems.

Above all, the seemingly unsolvable problem is the corruption that pollutes this project as well as many other development efforts in rural Uganda. It is clear to us that many of our Habitat committee members are mishandling the funds and taking advantage of their esteemed positions. There are way too many committees strung throughout this region where only four of us International Partners (IPs) are working. It's just too big and too much of a mess! Many of the committee members are getting frustrated with us – the Americans who hold the house-building money. They were so excited about our arrival because they expected to get their houses immediately.

So now that they see there is an accountability factor and that this program is intended for the common person in need, they are angry. The greed and manipulative behaviors have burst through the pleasant welcoming and hospitable nature of their initial interactions with us.

I miss you guys. I feel so lonely. I am lucky to have Bob and two other international staff to understand my woes, but they are suffering from the same disappointments. We have become cynical. We all left treasured friendships back home for an array of surface-level relationships that are blanketed by suspicion and mistrust. As far as we can tell, there is no appreciation for us being here. Even our management at HFHI is questioning the slow movement of this project.

They want to report to donors high numbers of Habitat houses and they seem less concerned about understanding the problems or the integrity of the program. Thus, we feel no support from the people we came to serve or from our supervisor.

Surely, things will get better. I just can't see it right now.

Love,

Carrie

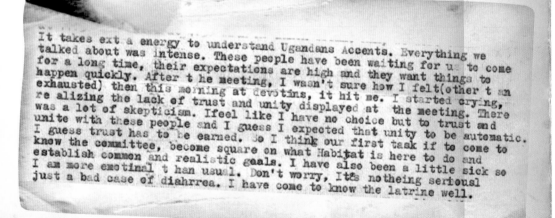

It takes ext a energy to understand Ugandans Accents. Everything we talked about was intense. These people have been waiting for us to come for a long time, their expectations are high and they want things to happen quickly. After t he meeting, I wasn't sure how I felt(other t an exhausted) then this morning at devotins, it hit me. I started crying, re alizing the lack of trust and unity displayed at the meeting. There was a lot of skepticism. Ifeel like I have no choice but to trust and unite with these people and I guess I expected that unity to be automatic. I guess trust has to be earned. So I think our first task if to come to know the committee, become square on what Habitat is here to do and establish common and realistic goals. I have also been a little sick so I am more emotinal t han usual. Don't worry, Itès notheing seriousl just a bad case of diahrrea. I have come to know the latrine well.

November 1991

Dear Caroline,

Some days seem like an eternity, even if I delay going out until midday. I am not able to sleep in because the loudspeaker at the local mosque begins amplifying prayers before daybreak. Then, the roosters chime in.

As the village comes to life, I know that someone will stop by to check on me, so I really do have to get up and dress. Sometimes I wish we hadn't hired Margaret to help with the laundry and dishes; I wish I could hide out in my house for a whole day and not see anyone! Other times, I know that I couldn't survive without her. Without plumbing in the homes, water must be hauled from a shared water pump 50 meters up the road. Margaret fetches the water and washes our dishes. She also washes our clothes once a week, taking them down to the river where there is lots of running water and big rocks to serve as drying racks. We wash our own dishes once a day and we wash some of our laundry. Margaret only comes for two hours a day. After weeks of trying to do it all, we figured out that if we did all of our chores without assistance, we would literally get nothing else done.

Caroline, I had told you that there are not many bugs here – well, there are. They are just different than the types of bugs at home. Of course, the biggest risk is the mosquitoes, which carry malaria. We stay protected from them by sleeping under a net and taking an anti-malarial prophylactic on a regular basis. The only downside to this medication is the nightmares. I often wake up (and wake Bob up) barking, for inability to let out a scream, because I have dreamt that an intruder has entered our home and is breathing heavily while hovering over our bed.

Remember when your parents used to tuck you in and say "sleep tight, don't let the bed bugs bite?" I always thought bed bugs were fictitious. They're not. We have bed bugs and they bite! Somehow they are not interested in Bob; they all go for my belly. It looks like I have chickenpox around my bellybutton. I went to the local drug shop, bought some diazanon and have soaked all sheets, mosquito net, clothes and just about everything in our house with this powerful "kill all" liquid. I even sprayed the walls in our bedroom. I was determined to kill those suckers!

While the bedbugs like me, the jiggers find Bob. Jiggers come from the dirt, and bury themselves in the tips of Bob's toes. There, they lay a sack of eggs. I get the surgical opportunity to dig them out with a needle. The challenge is to remove the sack without breaking it.

And then there is the tapeworm. The tapeworm lives happily in your intestines, eating whatever you feed it, and does not get excreted completely until it dies. Bits of worm are visible in bowel movements; however, because we have a long-drop latrine, we do not often see our deposits. I had one of these lovely creatures dwelling within me and only realized it when we were camping and had no latrine. The good news is that I could then treat for tapeworm, knowing what had been the source of my weight loss.

After I treated the tapeworm and got rid of the bedbugs, I thought I was good to go, but my illness saga continues. I thought my loss of appetite was simply because I could not bear to eat oatmeal mush for breakfast or peas and beans for lunch another day. I have experienced diarrhea for weeks on end.

Although most of my body is weak, my leg muscles have grown strong. I sometimes squat for hours a day over our little hole in the ground in our latrine. Last night, as I was squatting, half awake, half still in a dream, I wondered why there was a hose coiled up in the corner of the latrine. I dashed out when I realized the hose was a snake! I cried myself back to sleep.

Some days I just want to go home. What in the heck am I doing here? I don't have to be here. Why don't we just throw in the towel? We are wasting our time. We are sick and there is no hope for genuine sustainable development here. The fear and stigma of being a quitter is often the only thing keeping me here, besides Bob, of course. We made this commitment together. We will see it through together. We do love each other, though the stress of the situation is taking its toll on our relationship as well. I have not wanted to be touched by anything or anyone for months. This too shall pass.

Looking for better days,
Carrie

December 1991
Dear Bonnie,

As Christmas approaches, I must admit that I am feeling homesick. In many ways, I look forward to a simple Christmas without the overdone commercialism of the season back in the US. Actually, as I look out my window and see people hoeing their land, preparing to plant the next season's harvest, the thought of holiday hoopla makes me sick to my stomach. December around here looks pretty much the same as any other month. I'm glad to miss out on the over-scheduled days and excessive commercialism back home – that's not what I long for.

I miss family and friends. I miss being able to pick up the phone and call Mom, just to say "hi." I miss ice cream and chocolate chip cookies. I miss going out for a run. Yes, I could go for a run here, but I am already weird enough in the eyes of my neighbors.

Maybe my homesickness is just plain old sickness. I cannot seem to shake it this time. There are so many illnesses that result in diarrhea. Diarrhea is a common symptom for a variety of illnesses that require different treatments. We try to self-diagnose by using our trusty field guide – *Where There is No*

Doctor – which is exactly where we are! There is no doctor. My diarrhea is sometimes uncontrollable, meaning I do not always make it to the latrine in time.

On that happy note, Merry Christmas!!

Love,
Carrie

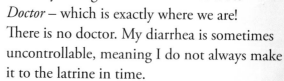

Journal Entry
February 1992

I cannot write letters home at the moment. There is no way to describe what I am experiencing in a way that family and friends will understand. Plus, I think my problems would worry my mother to death.

I have finally figured out my illness. With no doctors nearby, I have to do a lot of guesswork. I decided to take my stool specimen into the clinics in town. Being especially weak that day, I was so desperate that walking around Kasese town with my poop in a peanut butter jar did not even humiliate me.

I walked into the first clinic with my suspicious-looking jar and explained why I was there. The technician took my specimen and looked at it through his microscope. "Whipworm. It's definitely whipworm. I can prescribe the treatment," he said with authority. "Thank you very much," I said with relief.

As I was walking to the drug shop, (a closet-sized storefront on Main Street), still carrying my peanut butter jar, I saw another clinic. I decided to go and get a second opinion, even if it meant waiting in line again. This time my white face drew special attention and immediately someone said, "Can I help you?" While I often feel embarrassed by preferential treatment, that day I went ahead of three others and explained the purpose of my visit.

The technician took my jar to the back, came back ten minutes later and said, "I see nothing. You have common giardia."

"Are you sure? Please look again."

"I'm sure."

"Thank you very much. Is there another clinic in town?"

I went to yet a third clinic. What else did I have to do that day? Surely two out of three opinions would solve my mystery. "Could you please look at this under your microscope and tell me what I have?"

"This is definitely Amoebic Dysentery."

"What? No worms?"

"No worms, you have amoebas. I will give you a prescription to treat amoebas."

Walking out of the lab, I couldn't hold back tears; I was given three different diagnoses which require three different treatments. Taking all three would kill me – well, not really, but it would kill any good bacteria I had built up to fight other diseases. I pulled myself together and read for the umpteenth time the symptoms described in *Where There is No Doctor.* I made my decision, "It's got to be amoebas."

I have finished treating for amoebic dysentery. I am stronger, I feel better and I am beginning to regain my appetite.

My current sickness lies in my heart. I am just sad. I'm sad that a great program like Habitat for Humanity is such a misfit here. I'm sad that the wrong people are in leadership positions and that they are mishandling the money. I'm sad that we are not trusted and that we have no trust in our Habitat committee members either.

And I'm angry. I'm angry at God. We stepped out in faith that God would put us where we could make a difference, a place where we could learn and grow with the people. Instead, we are nobody's ally. Our boss will not listen to us, nor will the local Habitat committee.

My rage hit its breaking point when I burst into our house after another disastrous Habitat meeting. I went straight for the pots and pans. I threw them at our cement walls and started screaming at God. He had betrayed me.

He had led me into a situation that I couldn't handle and had let me down in such a big way that I began questioning His authority and power.

Sobbing uncontrollably, I ran outside to our

backyard and fell to the ground. I sat in our dustbowl of a garden and wept with my head buried in my knees for what could have been hours. When Bob came and tried to console me, I said, "Go away. This is between me and God."

My faith in the goodness of people had diminished. I was beginning to believe that the human race really is only self-serving, inconsiderate and godless. The few friendships I had developed felt tentative. I was unable to trust that love and kindness were genuine. I had sacrificed the joys of American living to serve in Uganda, and here I was, sick, disappointed, and ultimately hopeless. I thought God had promised to guide and protect me, yet I felt as though I had been slung through the mud and hung out to dry.

I don't know if I fell asleep or went deep into the realm of God, but I went somewhere. As my mind returned to the present, I lifted my heavy eyelids and looked up into the mountains that back-drop Kasese town. Long shadows stretched across the valley and I noticed that I was now sitting in a shadow cast by my little brick house. The rest of our yard remained in the warm glow of the late afternoon sun. It took me a few moments to come to my senses, but once I arrived, I knew that I had been fighting a spiritual battle, wrestling with God. I had surrendered – or more likely, God had graced me with peace. I was given peace to continue my walk in faith, peace that God would see me through. Somehow I knew that for me, leaving Uganda would mean letting Satan win the battle.

March 1992
Dear Caroline,

The recent storm of activities has been like a tornado that lifted us out of Kasese and dropped us in the village of Ibanda. We came pretty close to calling it quits and going home. In fact, had it not been for the Africa Area Director accepting our proposal to move to another village, we would have been on a plane by now.

Bob and I need a fresh start, an opportunity to develop a house building program with the right people, in an area that is the appropriate size for community development. Among all of the villages that we visited over the past several months, the committee in Ibanda seems to have people with integrity and commitment to service. Of course, like most in Uganda, they are poor farmers in need of better housing, but they have demonstrated extraordinary concern for each other and exemplary persistence in project startup. Bob and I both feel that Ibanda is where we are supposed to be.

We have spent the past two months helping to build our house, which is in the village trading center. The community has shown excitement about us moving here and choosing to work with them. Many volunteers have helped us with our house. It's starting to feel like Habitat again. We work side by side, laying blocks and painting, sharing lunch, and through the process, we are developing cross-cultural friendships and having a lot of fun. This is what we came to Uganda to do. This is a little slice of God's kingdom here on earth.

Looking back, I can see the downward spiral we were caught in. Perhaps we had to experience lots of ugly in order to appreciate beauty. God instilled in me a practice of looking for the good in people instead of focusing on the bad. I now realize that if you do not seek God, you may only find evil. Whatever the case, we are thankful to be in this beautiful place called Ibanda. We are once again hopeful for working with people in need to build simple, decent and affordable houses. We are once again excited to be in Africa, watching our journey unfold, trusting that it will become what it was intended to be.

Thanks for listening, Carrie

This epiphany, so boldly demonstrated in Uganda, and certainly one of the most important lessons of my lifetime, is a recent awakening for me. The depression that I experienced for six months in Kasese embodied my darkest days, my deepest valleys and my coldest heart. And, though I knew that God's grace had saved my pitiful state of being, I did not grasp the significance of the sequence of events. I did not understand that our valleys, followed by mountaintop experiences, are cyclical occurrences within an authentic relationship with God. I did not know, at that time, that I would walk through other valleys in life, having to depend on God's grace to be released from the darkness.

I suffered several depressions in the years following my return from Uganda. Those valleys, though not as physically challenging, were emotionally taxing, compounded by the guilt of knowing that Job and many others like him struggle to meet basic needs. I would think, "How can I be depressed? I have a good home, plenty to eat, a job, a loving husband. What in the heck is my problem?"

Each one of the depressions, sparked by varying circumstances, ran its course and resulted in a breakthrough of some sort: a new life chapter or a major decision unmistakably inspired by God. Still, I failed to recognize the importance of the battles.

My most recent depression was nine months before I started writing this book. I had experienced the vision for the book more than a year earlier and had buried the idea because of a lack of clarity and confidence. Fearing unknown territory, I tried to abort the project. I was in another spiritual battle, succumbing to the voices that said, "It's impossible. It's not practical. It does not make financial sense. There is no way you can plan a trip back to Uganda or publish a book."

This depression occurred during summer when I normally feel great. I expect winter blues and try to be proactive in keeping my spirits up. But this valley occurred right in the middle of my high season. We had a family vacation planned. The kids were out of school and all was well. There was nothing to complain about, no sickness, no worries. Still, I cried daily. My kids would ask, "Mom, are you crying again? What's wrong?" Embarrassed by my fragility, I would respond, "I don't know. I just need to cry."

I only understood the root of the depression once I came out on the other side. That fall I was preparing the photography exhibit, *Portraits of Uganda*. As I became entrenched in the images and the memories sparked by the faces, I began to have clarity about what had been stirring in me all these years. I realized that throughout the depression I had experienced the previous summer, God was preparing me for the task of writing a book. I had to become vulnerable, dependent once again on God. I had no answers, only questions. I had to believe that God would show me the way, if even only one day at a time.

That is exactly what He has done. As I face the challenges of writing a book, He gives me bits at a time. I call these bits "my daily bread." And more importantly, He gives me the stamina to continue this journey, even in absence of a complete map to the destination.

I gained new insight for this epiphany when I heard the song "Praise you in this Storm," by Casting Crowns. The song begins, "I was sure by now/God You would have reached down/And wiped our tears away/Stepped in and saved the day/But once again/I say "Amen,"/and it's still raining…"

The words pierced my heart. For the first time I understood that just because we call out to God during our suffering doesn't mean He will quickly relieve our pain or fix our ailment. He does, however, comfort us through our faith, giving us hope and strength to carry on. The song continues, "And I'll praise You in this storm/And I will lift my hands/For You are who You are/No matter where I am…"

Not only should I weather the storms in order to enjoy the rainbows on the other side, but I should actually be thankful during trying times; for it is my faith during trials that not only sustains me but carries me deeper into the presence of God. The Biblical Job's ongoing conversation with God demonstrated the personal nature of relationship that I should seek with my creator. Perhaps Job did not always show gratitude, but he always gave reverence to God, in spite of his doubting friends who ridiculed his faith.

I love the way Eugene Peterson captures the wisdom planted in the Book of Job. In his book, *The Message, Remix: The Bible in Contemporary Language*, Peterson comments on Job's direct communication with God. He begins the Introduction, "Job suffered. His name is synonymous with suffering. He asked, "Why?" He asked, "Why me?" And he put his questions to God. He asked his questions persistently, passionately, and eloquently. He refused to take silence for an answer. He refused to let God off the hook."

I am struck by how Job continued to wrestle with God, rather than cursing Him. After all, Job was an "upright" man, not one deserving the calamity placed upon him by God. Peterson continues, "Job gives voice to his sufferings so well, so accurately and honestly, that anyone who has ever suffered – which includes every last one of us – can recognize his or her personal pain in the voice of Job." Peterson commends Job for going to the top to protest his suffering, combating the bookish wisdom recited by his friends. Peterson writes, "Real faith cannot be reduced to spiritual bromides and merchandised in success stories. It is refined in the fires and the storms of pain."

Perhaps suffering brings forth wisdom – not book knowledge – rather heartfelt truths about ourselves, our world and our human frailties.

Authentic Friendship

There are many types of friendships: those based on similar life circumstances,
those formed around common interests and those inspired by intuition.
Friendships come in many shapes, sizes, and colors.
As long as a friendship is authentic, the type of friendship matters not.
An authentic friendship requires truth, vulnerability and genuine care.

Making and enjoying friends has never been a problem for me. Perhaps my upbringing nurtured the gregarious personality I inherited from my mother. Like her, I have always been drawn to a variety of people, interested in their life stories and appreciative of their different qualities. Life in Uganda presented new challenges to my natural ability to build relationships. But in the end, I was blessed with an expanded definition of friendship and an appreciation for folks who evolved from mysterious strangers into lifelong friends.

Truly great friends are hard to find, difficult to leave, and impossible to forget.

G. Randolf

Journal Entry
March 1992

Empowerment. Sustainable development. Dependency. Paternalism. Trickle down theory. Development from within. Oppression of the poor. The vicious cycle of poverty. These theories and realities come in waves, washing upon my shores – sometimes stormy, other times calm. Whatever the tempo, the steady suppositions color my social interactions, making it difficult to assess the potential for true friendship. Within my own culture, behavioral cues indicate the level of sincerity offered by another person. I am also blessed with an intuition that helps me see through the various masks that people hide behind. However, my intuition is worthless out of my own cultural context. I am unable to "read" Ugandans' intentions.

For many months, I have built walls around myself. I am afraid to approach friendship with local people because I feel that they are only seeking connection to the outside world. I am afraid that they are solely interested in what I represent. "Perhaps the American is a chance to get medicine, to get a Habitat house, for my children to obtain school fees…" I worry that if I seek friendship, my efforts will not be genuinely reciprocated. Then, I will be hurt and resentful.

The barrier between rich and poor separates us from our neighbors. They know as well as we do that our life with them in the village is temporary. If we choose to, we could hop on a plane and fly to the land of opportunity. This fact hinders my willingness to do the work necessary for developing authentic friendships. Unfortunately, withholding myself from other relationships causes me to be too dependent on Bob. At times, it seems we are each other's only friend, which is okay when we are in harmony but disastrous when in disagreement.

May 1992
Dear Caroline,

Thank you for your letters. You can't imagine how valuable letters from home are to us. They often save the day, reminding us that we have an abundance of love and support from lots of family and friends. Living in a culture so different from our own creates feelings of alienation and self-doubt. Reading letters from home comforts my soul and provides a place to escape into a sphere of familiar and cherished happenings. For three months we received no mail. It had gotten hung up somewhere and we thought we had been forgotten. Then one day, a backlog of mail and packages poured into town. Jackpot! It felt like Christmas Day!

As I think of you and other dear friends back home, I realize that my palette of relationships here is quite different. While Bob is certainly my best friend, I learned early on that he cannot be everything to me. I need girlfriends. I need my mom and my sister. Bob needs friends too. As much as I try, I simply have no interest in NFL football scores. During our first year in Uganda, Bob and I placed unrealistic expectations on each other. Our inability to meet each other's needs caused stress on our marriage. The positive outcome from our lack of other close relationships is that we both grew in our faith, filling the voids with prayer and lots of reading.

We have been forming new friendships with a variety of people. We have become good friends with Brent and Inell, a couple who are lifetime Baptist missionaries. Some of our best times have been visits to these American friends who live in Kasese town. We visit them every few months and simply savor the evenings. We enjoy catching up with each other's lives and doing American things. We sometimes make pizza and play board games. They have electricity, so we are able to watch videos. Recently we watched an NCAA basketball tournament game that had been recorded on a VHS tape and sent by Bob's parents. We also make ice cream and chocolate chip cookies. We often joke with them about expatriate friendships, in which the common ground rests in being foreigners. "Would we be friends in the USA?"

Well, considering they are from Michigan and we are from North Carolina, probably not. It makes our friendship somewhat of a cultural hybrid. Inell laughed when I told her I had never heard of rhubarb pie. She thought all southern women baked rhubarb pies.

We are certainly not attracted to all Americans. In fact, we are often repulsed by the American and European tourists who plow through the village with no respect or appreciation for the local culture. The other day, an open-top lorry (big truck) barreled up the dusty road, carrying tourists who had come to climb the Rwenzori Mountains. The women were sunbathing in bikinis! That is a shocking sight for rural Ugandans. I was embarrassed to be a mzungu.

There is a community of expatriates who are scattered throughout the region. Many of them are British, others are American and a few are from South Africa and Ireland. We each work for various non-governmental organizations (NGOs) and we differ in our religious beliefs and political opinions. But we share a common pull towards the needs in developing countries. This common interest, and again, the fact that we are all foreigners, is enough of a magnet for friendship. We share an understanding of poverty and development issues – topics that would have little relevance to our friends back home. Teasing each other about our various accents is fair game and we each own up to the strains of truth in the stereotypes that ridicule our precious homelands.

Calling anyone by phone is not an option since none of us have phones. So, when we see our expat friends, we tend to dive right into the thick of our lives, commiserating on the struggles and laughing at peculiar cultural incidents. Since there is really nowhere to go out, like to movies or dinner, we simply gather to cook and eat together, and occasionally trade books.

Once we met at a hotel for a retreat weekend. A luxurious hotel in its day (by Ugandan standards), the Tea Hotel in Fort Portal is a favorite spot for foreigners. Built in the 1950's, it is now a run-down facility which maintains the charm of a colonial lodge overlooking a vast tea plantation. The views from the grand veranda are magnificent, while the stillness is soothing to the soul.

Basic, but clean accommodations make this a great getaway (30 kilometers from our house.) Even though metal springs pop through the upholstery in some of the lobby furniture, the guest rooms are sparse, and electricity is more "out" than "on," our stay at this place feeds our hunger for comfort. Although there is not hot water from the tap, there are long, European-style bathtubs in the rooms. Every evening, the water-man knocks on our door and upon entering, shuffles through our room, carrying two buckets of boiling hot water to our bathtub. He fills the tub, and without saying a word, nods his head and leaves. Bob and I have stayed at this hotel several times and we always look forward to the water-man's knock on the door! We also intentionally reserve Room #5, the one that has a seat on the toilet.

Together with our friends, we ordered dinner by 2:00 in the afternoon so that it would be ready by 6:00. Then we enjoyed the afternoon sipping tea and/or beer on the veranda. We played cards, told jokes and stories, and relished being ourselves without onlookers taking note of the whacky wazungu. These expat relationships are treasured now and probably forever.

And then of course, there are our Ugandan friends. It is difficult to describe these friendships. Most of them are working relationships, as we tend to spend most of our time with Habitat committee members and Habitat homeowners. But they are also our neighbors. They are our cultural informants. They teach us how to live here: how to shop at the market, how to greet the elders, how to cook over a fire, how to pick stones out of our rice. We go on long hikes together, visiting families who have applied for a Habitat house. We cross rivers and blaze trails. They often interpret the language for us and explain to non-English speakers what the wazungu are doing in their village. In brief, they take care of us. The Habitat committee members feel responsible for our well-being and they make many efforts to assure our safety.

These cross-cultural friendships are not without challenge. Our Ugandan friends know that we have access to resources they do not. Bob and I seek the delicate balance between helping with the many problems inherent in poverty conditions, and creating unhealthy dependency relationships.

Of all our Ugandan friends and caretakers, Job Malighee has most captured my heart. Perhaps because of the amount of time we spend together (several hours a day), I have come to know him more personally than others. I enjoy his humble disposition and I respect his attention to learning. Job asks lots of questions, genuinely seeking knowledge, not the power that others in his position might seek. His quest for wisdom is grounded in his interest to better the lives of his family and his community. He demonstrates respect for elders, children, peers and strangers by his attentiveness and gestures; I've never seen him angry at anyone. Patience and integrity are but two of the virtues that I am learning by observing Job's conduct.

For example, Job often asks me or Bob to go to the bank to make the financial transactions. Because white people are given preferential treatment, I can be in and out of the bank within an hour, while a visit to the bank is an all-day event for Job. He sits and waits to be served in a room full of customers. Last week I grappled with whether to make the trip to the bank for Job. His tone was so respectful, nowhere near a plea; yet his argument was sound. We both knew that he was right about it taking him three times longer than it would for me to do the same task. We agreed to make the trip together and to slowly transition him into being the regular bank gofer.

Job often thanks me for all we are teaching him: project operations, bookkeeping, warehouse management, homeowner education. I smile and think, "Oh, if you only knew everything you are teaching us, just by being Job."

Thanks Caroline, for being a treasured friend, and keeping up with me and my musings over the distance.

Love you,
Carrie

Journal Entry
July 1992

The morning rays had not yet peeked through my wooden shutters, but something had woken me. I was savoring a recurring, but pleasant dream about vacation in the game park and relishing the comfort of Bob spooned to my backside. I heard scuffling outside of my window. Trying to remain asleep, I peaked through my eyelashes and saw our puppy, Rwanzo still curled up on the potato basket he has claimed as his bed. Someone was calling my name. A child, outside of our bedroom window, was trying to get my attention. I heard him whisper, "Keddy, Keddy…"

I got out of bed and slowly opened the shutters. There stood Mbusa, our nine-year-old neighbor. He doesn't speak much English but always manages to communicate with us. Mbusa lives with Betty and Mugisha, although he is not their son. I do not know the relationship between Mbusa and his foster parents, but it doesn't matter. Betty and Mugisha are his guardians.

"Betty is leaving," Mbusa whispered. Betty had sent him to deliver this news to me.

I was surprised that she wanted me to know. Betty's trust in me with such personal news was touching.

That was all Mbusa said and I didn't ask any questions. Details didn't matter. What mattered was that Betty was leaving and I should respond appropriately.

I quickly gathered some Ugandan shillings and gave the bundle of money to Mbusa to take to Betty. I didn't know where she was going or why she was leaving Mugisha, but I did know that she did not have any money.

I will miss Betty terribly. Our friendship is different from other friendships I have known, but it is special. Betty and I have had to search for things we have in common. I think we both decided that womanhood offers enough of a common base to spring from. I like her calm manner and I think she admires my creative energy.

I remember the first time I saw Betty. Crouched down in the front garden of our new house in Ibanda, she was uprooting the potato bulbs which she had planted in the unused land across the path from her tiny one-roomed shack. "*Wabukiri*," I greeted as I approached her. I learned later that Lukonzo is not her native tongue. Her mother was from the Bachiiga tribe and her father from Tanzania, but Betty has married into a Bakonzo family. I now greet her in Lugandan, a more widespread Ugandan language. There are other tribes represented here in Ibanda, though it is mostly Bakonzo territory.

"*Eh, Wabukiri*," she replied as she slightly bowed her head. Her smooth brown skin and timid eyes crafted a simple, yet stunning beauty. Her work clothes and head wrap did not steal her attractiveness.

"I am removing my potatoes from your land," she said as if she was embarrassed to have borrowed the plot.

"Oh, you can leave them. We will not plant anything until the next season," I replied with assurance that she had done nothing wrong.

Betty stood up tall and looked me in the eyes. This was the first time I saw her gentle spirit that I have since come to love. Her smile invited my friendship. I smiled in return, indicating my acceptance of her offer. We were complete strangers to each other, yet somehow we sensed friendship on the horizon.

"I'm Betty."

"Nice to meet you. I'm Carrie. Would you like to come in for tea?"

Betty is a neighbor and a friend. We greet each other every morning as we open our doors and windows, and begin our daily chores. I have taught her how to make American meals and she has taught me to cook African foods. We laugh at her baby, Benard and pass him back and forth to each other. Benard crawls around my house, getting into whatever he can find, which includes lots of papers and books. He also rolls around our cement floor with Rwanzo, who is now twice his size.

We have celebrated birthdays and Christmas with Betty and Mugisha. They have been so welcoming to us. I had no idea that Betty was unhappy in her marriage and certainly no prior indication that she was thinking of leaving. I guess we never really talk about those kinds of things. There is so much that we do not know about each other – so much that we couldn't understand about each other. I now realize that true friendship does not require details and that it can develop in spite of differences. It simply takes a little trust and mutual interest.

November 1992
Dear Mandy,

Hello dear sis! I miss you and hope you are doing well. I write today with thoughts about friendship. I have a choice to make. I can either keep Ugandans at bay, protecting myself from unrealized expectations for friendship, or I can let down my guard and give people a chance to know me – not as an American, but as a person. Though I have friendly relations with neighbors, I've not sought out deeper friendships like those I have with fellow Westerners. I think I would be happier and more fulfilled if I felt a stronger sense of belonging to this community.

One of my American friends, who lives in Kilembe (a 30-minute drive from us), has gone to Nairobi for an extended time. I did not see her often, but now I will not see her for months. She is undergoing therapy for depression. Her depression is steeped in circumstances that I know so well. I have felt the loneliness, the self-doubt and the angst that can be crippling to sojourners. And, probably more brutal than any of those feelings is the panic of being stuck in situations out of my control. I completely empathize with her and hope that the escape from cultural overload will refresh her spirit and give her new perspective. Her much-needed sabbatical to Kenya leaves me without a place for refuge. Her hospitality and comfortable American-style home has been such a safe haven for me.

We also recently said goodbye to two other dear friends, Habitat co-workers who had settled in distant but reachable parts of western Uganda. They are both single so they do not have the built-in companionship that Bob and I treasure. Perhaps they each developed much closer relationships with Africans than I have been able to – they would have had to rely on someone in absence of a spouse. But, the problems here are probably too intense to overcome without intimate support.

Anyway, I already miss them, if even just the comfort of knowing they were here in Uganda and that we would occasionally meet to enjoy friendship. David and Ellen are both significant friends to us; together we struggled through culture shock, depression, project failure and illness.

We also laughed together, sometimes uncontrollably, releasing tension and stress that had stirred up in each of us as we submerged ourselves into a world of unknowns.

I guess the reality is that the friendships I have depended on are now going to be distant. David and Ellen will be added to the long list of folks to whom I write letters. It is now time for me to transfer trust and intimacy to my Ugandan friends. They are the ones I am "doing life" with. It means peeling away a few layers and being vulnerable. I think I'm ready.

Women in the village are finally recognizing that I am not Wonder Woman. They have seen that I struggle with many of the same issues they do. We now talk about our female cycles, birth control, planting our shambas (gardens), and buying fabric for dresses. I think that they are beginning to see the real me, not masked by my American label nor my higher level of education. Women are recognizing that I too am a woman longing to have friends.

While the friendships with local women may look a little different than others of mine, they stem from the same base ingredient: authenticity. We care about each other and mutually trust that our cross-cultural relationships offer a whole new depth to life.

You may remember that my friend Betty had left home. She has returned and I am so happy. She was away for several months because her husband had failed to pay dowry to her family. I didn't understand the marital conflicts beyond this technicality, but I knew they had some things to work through while she was away. It is wonderful to have her back home and to continue building the friendship that we had begun.

Love you,
Carrie

Journal Entry
January 1993

My heart was beating like a drum. I looked at Job, Betty, Kumaraki and Bwanandeke and said, *"Tuwende!"* (Let's go) Our bed rolls, cooking supplies and duffle bags were all loaded in back of a 1981 Land Rover. We were headed up the mountain, where we would have a three-day planning retreat with our Habitat local committee.

Nobody was getting into the vehicle. Again I said with enthusiasm, *"Tuwende. Let's go, my friends!"* Still… blank stares. Finally, Job piped in, "But Carrie, do you know how to drive?" I then realized that not only had they never seen me drive but they had never seen a woman drive. In fact, it was only a handful of men from their villages who knew how to drive.

Trying to conceal my anxiety, I assured them that back home I drive all the time. What I didn't tell them was that the road conditions I am accustomed to are completely different: 1) Back home, we have paved roads, 2) Steep, curvy mountainous roads usually have shoulders and guard rails, and 3) Most stick shift cars have adequate gears, while this vehicle was somehow missing first gear!

The bottom line – I had no choice. I had to get these Ugandans up this mountain in this old rickety Land Rover – without a first gear. Bob had already taken another load of people and food up the mountain in another borrowed vehicle. Of course, there was no way to phone for help or choose some other arrangement. It just was what it was.

The drive up was not as bad as I had thought; it was worse. Single lane, dust flying, and loose rocks everywhere, especially as I oscillated between second and third to churn out enough power to swing the hairpin turns. Everyone, including me, gasped at the drop-offs revealed as we came around each bend.

We finally reached our destination just before dark. As we crested the last hill that took us onto the compound of an abandoned educational institute, I looked out at the beautiful vista surrounding us. I held back tears, full of relief for safe arrival and awe for the beauty of the land.

Bob and the committee members ran to the vehicle to greet us, hug us and help us offload our supplies. We were then welcomed with a hot meal. After a cup of chai and a bowl of warm rice and groundnut sauce, I was able to release the stress that had built throughout my body en route to this spectacular plateau in the Rwenzori Mountains of western Uganda. I was surrounded by those who had become our "family," people we had grown to trust and love. I had learned to live on the edge, trusting that God would offer provision and protection as He had done time, after time, after time.

The three-day retreat exceeded all of my hopes and expectations. Our Habitat management committee demonstrated the ability to think strategically, to act with genuine kindness, to share responsibility and most of all, to respect each other unconditionally. These are not things we have taught them; they are qualities that we gave them the space to unleash. Bob and I have clung to our conviction for development through empowerment. We have resisted continual temptations to move the Ibanda Habitat project along faster by doing many things ourselves. This retreat proved our steadfast approach to be worthy of the time invested. We have seen real leaders emerge to take ownership of their project.

We especially felt this affirmation when during the middle of the conference, Bob and I left the room so they could discuss a new management structure – one that would uphold the integrity of Habitat's mission but that would also be culturally and geographically relevant. When we came back into the room, we were pleasantly surprised to see a complete leadership plan: a plan not derived from our Western-world mentality, but one that would be understood by the local culture. We have learned from their wisdom and will take delight in watching their plan unfold.

While the meetings and logistics of meal preparation demonstrated a true team effort, Bob and I were most impressed that we, the wazungu, were equal team players. No longer were we the honored guests who sat separately, eating the delicacies of inner goat's parts, as in our early days in Uganda.

No longer were we expected to set the agenda, lead the meeting and explain Habitat policies and guidelines. We were now among peers, partners in a housing ministry. It was evident to us that the leadership of Ibanda Habitat for Humanity was resting in very capable hands.

That night as we split off into the girls' quarters and the boys' quarters for sleeping, I felt the peace that comes from being surrounded by friends – people whom I trust and respect. As we ladies prepared to climb onto our bedrolls, we giggled once again at our opposite habits. I took off my skirt to sleep in just my tee shirt, while they removed their blouses to sleep in just a slip.

My son often asks, "Mom, who's your best friend?" I respond, "Best friend for what?"

"You know, your best friend."

Although I know Adam would prefer a simple answer (one or two names would be adequate), I simply cannot answer his question without taking him into an expanded description of friendship.

For me, one friend may be best for a particular need or time in my life, while another friend may fit a completely different scenario. The idea of more than one or two "bests" seems to rattle his paradigm of friendship. After all, aren't we all supposed to be like Tom Sawyer and Huck Finn?

As you think about the friendships you have developed over the years, which ones hold lifetime value? What were the circumstances, the interests or attractions that sparked the relationships? What is the key ingredient that gives a relationship lifetime status?

For me, that ingredient is authenticity. That there is an element of "beneath the surface" sharing is crucial in determining the genuine nature of any friendship. Sometimes circumstances (occasionally crises) bring people together for short periods of time. Even within brief encounters, there is the potential for authentic friendship, where a particular need is met or a common purpose is shared. I have lost touch with many friends over the years; others have come in and out of my life once a decade or so. Being "lost-touch" friends does not, in any way, negate the authenticity of the friendship when it was active. In fact I haven't seen some of the folks on my list of lifetime friends in years.

An authentic friend is one who touches my heart and will be remembered forever. Most importantly, an authentic friendship means that the giver and/or receiver opened herself to honesty, vulnerability and genuine concern.

I am thankful to have learned in Uganda how to look beyond differences and find connection points for true friendship. Over the years, through our many moves, international travel and work assignments, I have formed and continue to nurture numerous friendships with a vast array of people. I treasure each and every one, as I think of the experiences we have shared and the lessons I have learned. Many of these friendships cross international, religious, generational and racial borders. Each of these friendships is unique, and all are based on authenticity.

Judgment

We are formed in the image of God. He created the world as diverse as it is big.
From the millions of plant and animal species to the enormous range of human
characteristics, God is the designer and master planner.
Therefore, let us not only tolerate differences, but embrace diversity
for the richness and balance that various cultures, races, and talents bring to the
strength and beauty of the human race.

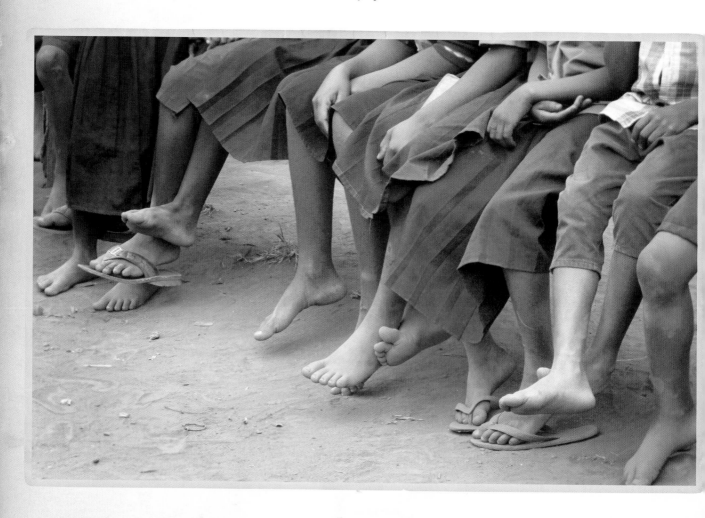

Somewhere deep inside each one of us is a broken spirit, perhaps mended, but delicate. That brokenness can result from a myriad of circumstances: lost loved ones, unmet expectations, failure, fear, rejection and discrimination.

Most, if not all, of the sources of human brokenness originate from us, the individuals who make up the human race. Though we are an intelligent, creative and resourceful species, we do wrong, most often to each other, but also to our planet and the natural resources provided to sustain our lives.

One of our most hurtful behaviors is the passing of judgment on others. This judgment is usually a result of our own ignorance or inherited hatred for another race, tribe, political affiliation or religion. One of the ugly facets of judgment is its divisive nature, which feeds other sins like greed, power and injustice.

Leaving the complexities of world conflict aside, I will focus in this chapter on a simple practice that each of us individually can strive for. The practice is to judge not, but rather honor diversity, seeking the wisdom buried in others' life experiences. Of course, passing judgment on others is a natural tendency. It is inherent for us to judge anyone who is different from ourselves. I am not referring to disagreement; we will always have differing opinions, beliefs and cultural lifestyles from others. I am challenging us to look beyond stereotypes, political affiliations and socio-economic structures we may not understand, in order to respect one another and seek "the god" in each person. Because somewhere deep inside of each one of us is a beautiful spirit.

If you judge people, you
have no time to love them.

Mother Teresa

November 1991
Dear Margaret,

So this is how it feels to be a minority: not only a minority, but an alien, a misfit, a fish out of water. I'm sure you are experiencing some of the same frustrations in Japan. I can imagine how you must stand out in a crowd, and I wonder what your appearance represents and communicates to the Japanese. "A white American woman teaching in Japan – she must be wealthy, smart, and highly educated. Is she unmarried?" What are the stereotypes that define you before you even open your mouth?

We come from a wealthy nation, the land of freedom and opportunity. The American label is difficult to shed. We are branded. And unfortunately, the wealth and glamor of movie stars defines the American lifestyle to most of the world. When I explain to Ugandans that there is also poverty, unemployment and illness in my home country, they think I am lying. There is no way for me to redefine what the American is to the rural African. Nope, I'm wrapped in a pretty white package, bulging at the seams with dollar bills and tied up with red and blue ribbons. The fact that Bob and I left lucrative careers to volunteer our service to Ugandans makes this distinction all the more frustrating.

But, I'm guilty too. My judgment of Ugandans stems from stereotypes as well. Americans generally believe that poor people are lazy and that the village guy should pull himself up by his own bootstraps and stop depending on aid from wealthy nations. The tribalism, polygamy and subsistent lifestyles still prevalent in African societies represent to Westerners an unwillingness to progress or develop into more productive and efficient communities.

These are the walls I hope will crumble as we seek cross-cultural relationships, although at this moment, I am dispirited. As I was walking home from the market today, I felt discouraged. I had been overcharged for my produce because I didn't have the energy to bargain for every peanut and tomato. (When my white face appears at the market, somehow the prices of everything double.) Today, all of the beggars' hands landed in front of me – I felt singled out – and what is usually a soft heart for any need, was closed to all.

I sometimes wonder what it would be like if I were an African American, able to conceal my identity beneath my skin, if even momentarily, until I opened my mouth and spoke with my American accent.

As we came through Queen Elizabeth National Park recently, we took a game drive to see elephants and hippos. We stopped our vehicle to watch a herd of elephants feed on the fruit trees. It was a peaceful, beautiful moment, backdropped by an African sunset. That is, until the largest elephant took notice of us. He began flapping his ears and stomping his feet. He swung his trunk in disapproval of our presence. Submissive to his power, we threw the Land Rover in reverse and backed out of his space. After the scare and as we were driving out of the game park, I thought, "I know how you feel big guy; it's not fun to be watched all the time!"

I hope you are enjoying your time in Japan. I look forward to sharing stories with each other in a couple of years.

All the best,
Carrie

Journal Entry

January 1993

Today goes down in my history book. It was a historic day for Kasese town, but for different reasons than my personal experience.

Pope John Paul II visited Kasese today. While Catholics make up almost half of the primarily Christian population, Catholicism is but one of the many faiths practiced here. The Church of Uganda (Anglican), Seventh Day Adventists, Church of Christ, and Baptists are active denominations in this area. Muslims comprise about a tenth of the overall population, but their wardrobe (white gowns and head coverings) stand out, making them seem more prevalent. Even though most Bakonzo people have chosen the Christian or Muslim faith, their cultural history is grounded in traditional beliefs (animism and witchcraft), and those practices seep into their lives, regardless of their faith. From an American Christian perspective, the mixture of traditional beliefs and church-imposed systems is an interesting anthropological study.

We were interested in seeing the Pope simply because he's the Pope. We were not seeking his blessing, or his words of wisdom; our curiosity drove our desire to witness the visit by the head of a major world religion.

Yesterday we traveled to Kasese and spent the night with friends who live on the edge of town. The preparation for the VIP visit began early this morning as they set up the stage, decorating with banana trees and palm branches. Announcements, broadcast over a loud speaker from the Catholic Church, echoed through town as the preparation progressed. Knowing that big events consume the whole day in African time, we were in no hurry to walk to town. Instead, Bob and I enjoyed a nice leisurely morning at a home with electricity. Homemade waffles and piping hot coffee! We even watched TV. We were not concerned about getting a seat at the event since our intent was to stand in the back and take in the whole experience.

Around noon, Bob and I walked to town, following a sea of brightly dressed Ugandans making their way to the big gathering.

Women were dressed in the traditional *basuti*, a long dress made of silk or polyester. Pleated, puffed-up shoulders and a big cummerbund distinguish the Ugandan style of dress. I wore my best dress, which is not a basuti, but is made out of African fabric.

When we reached the top of the hill that overlooks Kasese town, I couldn't believe how many people filled the valley. There were tens of thousands. Of course, this was an outdoor event in the heat of dry season—no shade and standing room only by the time we arrived. Weaving through streams of people, we made our way down into the valley and found a place to stand where we could see the stage but also an array of activity that surrounded the event.

I was enjoying photographing people, capturing the energy they displayed as they sought inspiration from their religious leader. Many of them hoped for healing; others sought blessings from the anointed one. I came to experience culture and get good photographs. It was only minutes after we settled into our spot when an official approached us, took our arms and began escorting us towards the stage. When we inquired what he was doing, he simply responded, "You come."

The man took us through rows and rows of people and then handed us to another escort who took us up another 20 meters where he passed us along to another escort. With each escort, we said, "We are not officials. We are residents, not special visitors."

"You come."

I began to fear what this process was leading to. Perhaps they had mistaken us for Catholic missionaries and would expect us to perform some ritual on stage!

The first ten rows of seats facing the stage were ribboned off with signs that read, "Distinguished Guests Only." Seated in this section were white people mixed in with government officials we recognized. Our guide politely extended his arm and nodded his head, indicating the reserved seats for us, the *Distinguished Guests*.

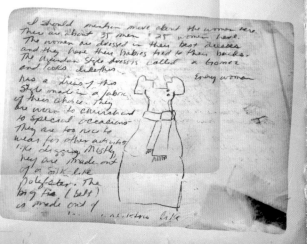

The lump in my throat was too large to swallow. While I was embarrassed to re-ceive recognition and VIP treatment because of my white skin, the section of seats offered to us was the only one shaded by a tent. The midday sun was scorching my fair skin and I was already beginning to feel weak. The Red Cross could not hand out water fast enough to keep people from passing out under the hot sun.

There we sat, fifteen feet from the Pope. And there I was: a protestant, taking a highly coveted seat.

As the ceremony progressed, the Pope's words became a murmur to me as dark-ness smothered my vision – not because of my guilty feeling, but because of the heat. I whispered to Bob, "The monkeys are getting me," which he understands to mean that I am experiencing heat exhaustion. I was conscious, but all I could see was blackness and my skin became clammy.

The rest of the event is a blur to me. Although I heard voices and some singing, I continued to see only stars as we left town, Bob guiding my every step back to the house. I have rested and am feeling better. This was one of several heat-related illnesses I have experienced here, so it was not too much of a scare, nor is it the main point of the story.

The historical relevance of today for me is about being treated with ultimate respect based on an assumption. And while it feels much better to be regarded in a higher position than to be looked down upon, it's the same injustice. I kept think-ing of African Americans being sent to the back of the bus before the civil rights movement in the US, and all the other atrocities based on racial discrimination. To be treated differently based on skin color, for better or for worse, is unethical.

May 1993
Dear Mandy,

Every ride on public transport generates a story, a lesson learned or a perplexing brush against the culture. Today I hopped on the back of a pickup truck going from Ibanda to Kasese. The driver stuck his arm out the window and motioned for me to come to the front. Oftentimes, when there is room in the cab, the driver lets me ride up front. It's still a squeeze, as there are usually four people in the front, but we do get to sit down. Others offered a seat in the cab of the truck are older men, pregnant women or women with small babies.

I often end up beside the driver, with the gear shift between my legs. Nobody besides me seems to think it's funny that the driver shifts from first to second to third with his hand on the knob which sits between my knees. Nor do they seem to notice when the key falls out of the ignition when we're driving. The driver keeps on driving while he reaches down to pick up the key. I never cease to be amazed at how things are jerry rigged.

In Kasese I boarded another matatu headed to Hima. Bob and I oversee the Hima Habitat project as well as this one in Ibanda. This simply means that we visit them once a month, check their accounts and meet with the executive committee.

Thankfully I wasn't the first one in the matatu; these things sit parked until they fill up. There is no particular schedule – when it's full, it goes. I was the second one on my bench, which meant that there was room for one or two more people. Over the course of an hour the matatu filled: all but the seat next to me. There was obviously an open seat, but the last passenger in sat in the row in front of me, making that seat four to the bench.

I couldn't figure out why that man squeezed onto the bench with three people, instead of sitting next to me. I held my bag on my lap trying to offer as much space as possible. Perhaps my squinted brow revealed my thought, "why didn't he sit next to me?"

The man on the other side of me leaned toward me and whispered, "That man is a Muslim. He cannot sit next to a woman who is not his wife."

"Oh, I see," I responded.

When we came to our first stop to offload and pick up passengers, a tall, very thin man got in and sat next to me. I found myself analyzing him. His features were pointed, not round like the Bakonzo people. His skin was dark, almost black. I guessed that he was Karamajong or one of the other nomadic tribes from the northern part of Uganda.

Then, my mind got stuck on his skinniness and I decided that he must have AIDS. It is estimated that one in twenty Ugandans are infected with HIV/AIDS. They call it the skinny disease.

My assumption about the man sitting next to me fueled my anxiety about this terrible disease that is sweeping the continent. With every bump in the road, our sweaty arms touched as we bounced from side to side. I was extremely uncomfortable. My thoughts went berserk as I imagined having a car accident. The crash would cause our blood to mix and I would become infected with AIDS.

How ABSURD! Isn't it just awful that we judge strangers?!? I didn't know a thing about this man, yet I had decided that he was dying of AIDS and that sitting next to him posed a threat to my health as well.

After several hours in Hima with the committee, I caught a ride back to Ibanda. Tired and culturally exhausted, I had no energy to think. On the ride back home, I closed my eyes and allowed myself to meditate, "All ears, God. Go for it."

He filled my heart with Joy. Not happiness, but with Joy, a friend who is suffering from AIDS. She is an incredible Christian. She lives on faith and shares openly with others. Surviving this illness has put a new dimension to her walk with Christ. Joy has been an inspiration to me as she demonstrates reliance on God for hope and healing. And that she has the courage to tell people about her illness is a testimony of her faith. Joy also lives up to her name, as she radiates the grace of the Holy Spirit in her kindness to others.

Speaking about AIDS is culturally taboo in Uganda. When people die of AIDS, the cause is usually attributed to a tragedy or some other malady. However, to Uganda's credit, President Musevini has owned up to the pandemic and is leading a nationwide education and awareness program about HIV/AIDS.

Even though I felt like a schmuck for plastering a label on the skinny man and feared contact with him, I appreciated God using the experience to remind me of respect: respect for Muslims and their cultural practices, respect for people with illness, respect for people I do not understand and respect for people that judge me out of their preconceived notions.

I write from the comfort of my own bed – so thankful to have learned another lesson and ever grateful that the day is done. My bed never felt better.

Missing you,
Carrie

Journal Entry
February 1994

Matthew 7:1 "Do not judge, or you too will be judged."

Matthew 7:3, "Why do you look at the speck of sawdust in your brother's eye and pay no attention to the plank in your own eye?"

Good question, Jesus. Why do we judge others? If we're not judging someone by the color of their skin or their nationality, we're ridiculing them for a religious belief or a cultural practice. We look at a person's tattoos, tattered clothes or fine jewels and make assumptions about their decisions or intentions. Our generalizations about people are a result of attitudes and behaviors that we have learned from our parents and other influential people in our lives.

So, just maybe, we need to be judged and feel the pain, frustration and rage associated with being the victim, in order to recognize that we (every one of us) are at times the culprit.

Recently I caught myself being judgmental of one of our committee members. He and a young woman I didn't know stopped by the house on their way home. It was getting late and darkness was setting in. I had met his wife, and this wasn't her. He explained that this was his new girlfriend, soon to become his second wife. When he asked if they could stay the night and continue on their way in the morning, I responded, "No, I don't think that's a good idea."

Culturally, polygamy is still common. He didn't understand my disapproval, but I just couldn't get beyond my discomfort with the situation. These culture clashes often cause unfair conclusions about people's behaviors and character.

Another recent experience demonstrates my judgmental nature. Bob and I were working in our backyard. Bob was mixing cement to use for plaster for the interior walls of our house in Ibanda. I was shoveling sand from a pile into the wheelbarrow and hauling it to Bob to mix into the cement. Any time I use a shovel or hoe, or any tool for that matter, villagers seem to be entertained. It has become clear that they have never seen a white woman do hard labor. In fact, they have not seen a white woman do much of anything because there have been few white women in this rural part of Uganda.

So when snickers surrounded me and my wheelbarrow, I was not surprised, just slightly irritated. I said to Job, who was helping us with our house that day, "What do they think white women do?"

"They have only ever seen white women dressed smartly and riding in the front seat of vehicles."

"Well, let this be a lesson," I replied with a bit of a snotty attitude, though slightly in jest. I dug the shovel even deeper into the pile of sand.

As I continued to work, I noticed an old woman with a big load on her back, walking down the road. When she reached a place in the road where she could see me, she stopped and watched me for awhile. Her face carried many wrinkles. Her bare feet and hands were worn and callused. I couldn't read her expression, so I created my own idea of what she was thinking. I decided that she was perplexed by my role as a woman – having no children and only two rows of vegetables in my garden, "What's the muzungu doing here anyway?"

I tried to conceal my thoughts behind a friendly, "*Wasibiri Mama*" (Good afternoon ma'am).

"*Eh, Wasibiri,*" she replied as she turned to continue her journey.

A few moments later, I noticed that she had come back. This time, she had outstretched arms, offering us two sticks of sugarcane. "*Wasinga Erikola,*" (thank you for the work) she said as she gave us the sugarcane. Then she tied her remaining four stalks of sugarcane back on top of her sack of cassava and slowly walked on.

I felt like a crumb. What respect, gratitude, and humility she had demonstrated to me after I had assumed she was judging my inadequacies.

Forgive me God. I am still learning.

A brief encounter with someone often produces the most critical judgment. A glimpse of someone's behavior, condition or outward appearance can steer our minds into a myriad of untruths. And if we have no personal experience with the cultural characteristic or action that we judge, we are most likely wrong in our assessment.

We're all guilty of this. Who do we judge? An obese person, a skinny person, a homeless guy, the parents of a child throwing a temper tantrum, a conservative Christian picketing for a cause, a teenager tattooed from head to toe, a lesbian, a republican, a democrat, a Catholic, an Arab, a mother yelling at her children, an absent father, a smoker, a person with AIDS, an alcoholic, a wealthy person, a prostitute, a person with mental illness, a bragger, a bigot – the list goes on.

Are you still innocent? Not me; I have passed judgment on many of those people. Here's more – a self-righteous person, a Jehovah's Witness, a Mormon, a breastfeeding mom, mixed-raced children, a migrant worker, a motorcycle man, parents with lots of children, a couple with no children, a war veteran, missionaries, missionary kids, a naturalist, a gambler, a drug addict – I could go on forever with our labels.

What boat have you been in? What was your family situation? What environments have you either fallen into or chosen to explore?

We are influenced by our environments and the people who fill our lives. We take on new roles, develop opinions and try different lifestyles. Sometimes we have the privilege to choose our paths, and many times we cannot see the choices available to us. Some of our choices enhance our health and wellbeing while other choices are harmful. Our choices are judged by other people, as are the circumstances that are out of our control.

Reserving judgment on others is a life-long challenge. While in the Christian faith we are encouraged to "speak the truth in love," (Ephesians 4:15) we are also commanded to "love our neighbors as ourselves." (Mark 12:31). Condemning others is not a task that Christ Jesus has given his followers. Sadly, American Christians have a reputation for being judgmental, self-righteous and exclusive. Isn't it ironic that Christ Jesus taught about unconditional love, yet many of his followers have crawled into a self-serving box that shuts out people who don't fit their church ideals? We (Christians and non-Christians) judge out of our own ignorance and fears. Thankfully, God washes us with His grace and gives us fresh opportunities to grow beyond our human tendencies.

In Hindi, the term *namaste* means "I greet the god in you." What a beautiful way to look beyond stereotypes. A simple bow of the head and greeting with this honorable word demonstrates the respect for the spirit which dwells within, often deep beneath layers of stereotypes. Though I only use the term namaste in my yoga practice, I strive for the discipline to seek beneath a person's outside layers.

My mom always said, "Mind your own business" and "follow the golden rule," "Do unto others as you would have them do unto you. (Matthew 7:12) That sums it up. It's about respect. We may not like another's life choices or cultural behaviors, but we can respect the individual, knowing that she or he was uniquely created by God. We have many gifts – some developed and recognized and others yet to be tapped.

This epiphany of embracing diversity rather than practicing judgment solidified in me during a Habitat International training event in Asia. I had spent the week with people from seven Asian and Pacific countries – including the Philippines, Korea, New Zealand, and Papua New Guinea – countries that represent a wide spectrum of cultural differences. We had spent the week wrestling with common development issues. We had shared training strategies and methodologies. We had sampled the many different foods from their countries, had sung songs in different languages and had talked about Christian, Buddhist, Muslim, and Hindu values. I had shared a room with an Indian girl who was promised in marriage to her uncle. While physically working on a Habitat house together was a highlight for everyone, I most enjoyed working diligently with a cross-cultural team to develop training modules which would be effective in intercultural settings.

As we stood in a big circle holding hands at the end of our week, we celebrated the work we had done. We celebrated our many cultures. And mostly, we celebrated the grace of God.

That grace washed through me, offering forgiveness for all past judgments I had made on people. And it brought a promise of continual forgiveness for the rest of my life. I am so fortunate to have been given an opportunity to experience a slice of the world. I honor the complexity and diversity of a world that only the creator can understand.

Millard Fuller, the founder of Habitat for Humanity, coined the expression, "Theology of the Hammer," which means people working together for a common cause, in spite of their differences. Millard said, "…differences of opinion exist on numerous subjects – political, philosophical, and theological – but we can find common ground in using a hammer as an instrument to manifest God's love."

One of the beauties in service to others is that working together for the betterment of life conditions unifies people from different walks of life. The rich work with the poor, Christians work with Muslims, Democrats work with Republicans, blacks work with whites, Africans work with Americans, and so on. Perhaps one of God's purposes in creating such a diverse world was for us to learn from others and to love one another unconditionally.

For God did not send his Son into the world to condemn the world, but to save the world through him.

John 3:17

Peace that Passes Understanding

We wrestle with major decisions. Ultimately, we want to do what is best for ourselves, our families and those affected by our decisions. Best does not always mean easiest or most practical. The best decisions are those made from the heart, with peace in our spirit, no matter the outcome or perceived success.

There were two distinct parts of our overseas term. We often refer to these as "the before" and "after," much like the way we describe the "pre-kids" and "after-kids" phases of our marriage. In Uganda, we acquired three commodities, all at about the same time: these three possessions defined the "after" portion of our term. The pressure lamp, the gas oven, and the dog made the difference between mere survival and a pleasurable daily life. Had we known how much these things would enrich our simple lifestyle, we would have acquired them much earlier than halfway through our three-year term of service.

Do not be anxious about anything, but in everything, by prayer and petition, with thanksgiving, present your requests to God. And the peace of God, which transcends all understanding, will guard your hearts and your minds in Christ Jesus.

Philippians 4:6-7

December 1993

Dear Mom and Dad,

Thank you for your letters. It's wonderful to hear about things back home. We are so settled into our life here that I rarely think of American settings any more. I used to dream about going home. For example, once I dreamed that I went home and ended up at Park Road Shopping Center. I didn't have a car, so I called home from a pay phone booth and asked for someone to come and pick me up. Woody answered the phone and said, "I don't have enough room in the van for you." Of course, here, they can always squeeze in another passenger, or goat or whatever you are hauling. I was livid at his response.

Another time I dreamed that I phoned home to Mandy from Kampala. As we were talking she said, "Hold on, Mary Claire is crying."

"Who is Mary Claire!?"

"Didn't I tell you that I had a baby?"

My dreams revealed some of my fears about being away from home for so long. I was afraid that we would eventually be completely forgotten.

Those fears have subsided and now my dreams revolve around African adventures and our daily lives. I write to you today from a place of peace. We are happy and so grateful to live in this beautiful setting. Rainy season brings fresh air and crisp mornings. People are cheerful and moving about the village with energy, trying to get in the day's work before the afternoon rain sets in. The flowers in our front garden are vibrant and full, especially the hollyhocks that we planted by our front door. They have grown tall enough to look me in the eye and greet me with their fluffy pink blossoms. Our green grass complements the red and pink beds that border our reed fence.

As we walk to Nora's to get fresh baked bread, we look up at the snow-capped peaks of the Rwenzoris.

Having climbed the Rwenzori Mountains twice now, the "Mountains of the Moon" are no longer a mystery to us, but rather a majestic marvel.

After trekking through bogs, forests, rivers and boulders for four days, the ascent up the glacier with ice axes and crampons to reach Margherita Peak was much more than a natural high. At nearly 17,000 feet, Margherita Peak is the third highest in Africa. From the jagged, pointy top, we looked east to Uganda and west to Zaire. The four-day trek back home was full of awe for what we had seen and anticipation for returning to our bed! I now understand why people come from all over the world to climb the Rwenzori Mountains; this range truly is amazing in its grandeur, unique in its vegetation and rugged with splendor. And we live right here at the base of these incredible mountains!

In addition to our picturesque surroundings, the simplicity of our lifestyle contributes to our wellness. The less you have, the less you have to worry about. I often delight in not having to pay bills, not having to choose which things to buy, and not having to meet tight deadlines. We are content with a few simple pleasures. We recently bought a pressure lamp and a gas oven. Simple as they are, these appliances have added much enjoyment to our days. I don't know why we waited so long to get a pressure lamp – maybe because they cost $40. That's pricey for our meager monthly stipend. And, we were quite okay with candlelight. It always meant early to bed, early to rise. But now we extend our evenings, playing cards and reading to the wonderful light provided by our pressure lamp, which illuminates our whole living room. Now I find it amazing that we did everything, including dinner clean-up, by the dim light of a candle.

The oven – well, that's a story. "Where in the heck did you get a gas oven?" you might ask. Missionaries in Kampala, friends of friends, were selling all of their housewares before leaving the country. So, we decided to buy the gas oven. Getting this appliance to Ibanda was the real trick. We combined our trip to Kampala to fetch our oven with collecting our friend Rich, who had come to visit us. We rented the Habitat double-cab pickup and used the vehicle during Rich's holiday with us.

On our way home from Kampala, just for fun and adventure, and because this was one of the few times we actually had a vehicle, we took the long way through Queen Elizabeth National Park. We hoped to see the tree-climbing lions that reside on the Ishasha side of the park.

The long way ended up being the wrong way. Because of the heavy rains, the road had washed out into a slip-sliding mess, for miles. There were lorries stuck on the sides of the road and few vehicles could muster enough power to push through the mud. Every bump, twist and slide that jolted our truck sent the oven tumbling, sliding and banging in the bed of the truck. We wondered if there would be anything left of the oven when we arrived home.

We slept the night in the park at the ranger's station and enjoyed some campfire stories with the ranger, who graciously gave us a tent to sleep in as well as permission to camp for the night. The following day, we navigated the roads to complete the journey home. We did see tree-climbing lions, as well as a lake filled with hippos. At first glance, we thought the hippos were massive rocks poking through the water's surface. Once the symphony of snorting began, we became aware that plunked in muck before our eyes was partial proof of Uganda's global claim of "most bio-mass."

Also on the way home, we visited the Bwindi Impenetrable Forest, an area that hosts mountain gorillas. We took a short hike and though we did not find the gorillas, the adventurous nature of the search was worth the walk.

When we arrived home, our oven was in pieces. All knobs and screws had come loose and the oven door was completely off its hinges.

Everything can be fixed. It might not look like it used to, but our oven works like a charm. With a four-burner stove on top and an oven, we cook multiple entrees and bake cookies simultaneously! We haul the gas cylinder to Kasese town for a refill once a month.

I cannot even begin to express how this cooking convenience has enhanced our life! We now enjoy cinnamon toast and hot coffee for breakfast instead of oatmeal and lukewarm coffee.

At first I was embarrassed for neighbors to see our oven. I felt rich and privileged. Bob knew that I was sensitive about owning this sign of wealth and he enjoyed teasing me by peeking into the kitchen window from outside and saying, "Hey, what you got there? Is that an oven?"

Now, I simply enjoy baking and sharing cakes and cookies with friends. As it turns out, it really isn't a big deal. Our neighbors expect white people to have much more than themselves, and they appreciate the tasty baked goods.

Bob, Rwanzo and I are three peas in a pod. We are happy. Life is good. We enjoy the days much more since we have scaled back our expectations. Somehow we have peace within ourselves that we are supposed to be here, even though we don't understand all the reasons why. Perhaps God needed to teach us a few lessons about patience, grace and humility before He could open our hearts to joy and gratitude.

Since we moved the Habitat office out of our house (about a month ago) we are enjoying a little privacy again. Job is no longer coming to our home every morning; instead we meet him down the road at the new Habitat office. Also, Habitat homeowners, who make their house payments with building materials instead of cash, are hauling their roofing sheets and bags of cement to the office instead of to our front door!

Our evenings are simple and relaxing, as we play cribbage, write letters, read about future vacation spots, and play with our dog. Rwanzo rests his head in my lap as I write. Perhaps he is the heartbeat of our joy. I never anticipated becoming this attached to a pet.

Love you, Carrie

December 1992
Dear Mark and Anne,

We are the proud parents of a dog, the most beautiful dog in the Rwenzori Mountains. The story goes like this:

"Bob, Bear had puppies again. Should we look at them?"

"Carrie, you know as well as I do that it doesn't make any sense for us to have a dog. We will get too attached and then have to leave it behind when we go back to the States."

"You're right. But wouldn't it be nice to have a little puppy to cuddle? Okay. No dog – it was just a crazy idea."

Two weeks later I just happened to be in Kasese, visiting our missionary friends who own Bear, a pure African mutt. There were three puppies left. Reluctantly, and feeling kind of naughty, I said, "I'll take this one, the golden brown pup with the ridge up his back. He seems to be the most playful." Little did I know that a playful puppy often grows into a rambunctious, WILD, dog.

The ride back to Ibanda was even more tedious than usual. I was used to standing in the back of a pickup truck with 12-15 other passengers, letting my body sway and swoop to the rhythm of the potholed roads. Only when I am carrying fresh eggs am I concerned about cargo. This trip was different. I now had a precious little bundle of fur with two brown button eyes, looking to me, his new mom, to comfort and protect him.

I was thinking, "Bob is going to kill me for bringing home a puppy, but I sure want to at least get this pup home alive. Surely, Bob will come around."

And he did. I think it took about ten minutes for Bob to completely fall in love with the puppy. I was thrilled to see the way he cared for our new puppy; what a great dad my husband will be. We showed our puppy to Betty and Mugisha, our neighbors, asking them for name ideas.

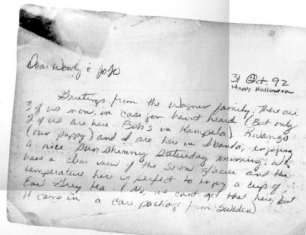

Surely only a Lukonzo name is appropriate for this dog of the Rwenzori Mountains. Betty came up with *Olhuonzo* (Americanized to Rwanzo) which means beloved. Betty sensed how special this dog is to us. I think she has grown fond of him as well.

Bob took the lead role in Rwanzo's training and has been spending twenty minutes a day doing training sessions. He walks around our yard and the village trading center with Rwanzo on a sisal rope (usually used for tying goats) and practices over and over, "Sit. Stay . . . Rwanzo, Come!" I am enjoying watching the two of them build friendship. My training sessions with him are much less successful than Bob's. One day I beat the tar out of him with a rolled-up magazine because I got so mad at him for not obeying anything I commanded him to do! I hope this is not an indication of the kind of parent I'm going to be!

Bob needs a dog. He needs true companionship in the way that only a dog can give. And even if we have to bid farewell to Rwanzo when we leave Uganda, the joy he provides now will be worth the sorrow we will experience in leaving him. I hope all is well in Charlotte. We miss you guys.

Love,
Carrie

Journal Entry
January 1993

Our yard boy, Tom, said, "Rwanzo's a happy dog." That comment struck me as funny. I mean, aren't dogs generally happy? What's there not to be happy about? I started taking notice of other dogs around the village to understand Tom's comment. Mostly napping in the shade, the other dogs were not out romping around, chasing goats and dragging home cow horns the way Rwanzo does. I think Tom meant that Rwanzo is active. He was right; our little Rhodesian Ridgeback mix is certainly active!

When Rwanzo gets that look in his eye, we know it's coming. It starts with a short bark, just once. Then he cuts his eyes sideways and gives the "I dare you to chase me" growl. Suddenly, the raucous play begins. Tail in the air, down on his front elbows, he barks up a storm as he shakes his head back and forth; he will not accept no for an answer. After he has stolen your full attention, he darts around the yard, running in a figure eight like he is being chased by a cheetah. We refer to these moments of madness as "the dog devil has gotten hold of him." Once Rwanzo has thoroughly exhausted himself (usually in about ten minutes), he crawls into our laps, all 60 pounds of him, and takes a nap.

Our beautiful, distinguished dog makes an impression on people. They know he is no ordinary dog. Rwanzo is a handsome dog and he carries himself like royalty, displaying courage and confidence. The children are as curious about him as they are afraid of him. He generally stays within our three-foot-high reed fence that surrounds our home. But when he wants to explore something on the other side, he finds a gap in the fence created by reed snatchers, people who sneak a few reeds from the fence for firewood. Children often sit on the outside of the fence, peering through the gaps, watching Rwanzo as if he were an animal in the zoo. Rwanzo sometimes runs towards the kids to give them a little scare, and then he dodges the rocks hurled at him by the children just before they run away screaming.

As if we wazungu are not enough of a spectacle in this village, the addition of a rambunctious dog following behind us provides great entertainment for the children. Rwanzo bounces along, occasionally flitting into the bush. Then he pops back onto the trail, wagging his tail in delight at the banana peel or mango pit he has found. He chases after chickens and goats, just for the fun of it. One time, he created a disastrous situation as he chased a goat into the river. Bob rushed into the gushing water to grab the goat as he rapidly swept by. Rwanzo barked as a large audience cheered at the river's edge. I didn't know whether to laugh or cry. Truly, this dog, though he infuriates us with his naughty behavior, is a delightful addition to our lives. He makes us laugh and spend less time worrying about problems we can't fix.

Rwanzo offers such companionship and protection. Bob is currently in Sweden to be in his friend Patrick's wedding. Rwanzo and I are on our own for the week. He snuggles in my lap as I read and write. His soft brown fur collects my tears when I'm sad and his alert expressive eyes indicate his excitement when I'm ready to play tug of war with a knotted sock.

I have to admit that I have fallen in love with this dog.

April 1994
Dear Rich,

The place we called home for three years is now an exit stamp in our passports. As we travel through Africa and Asia, transitioning ourselves to a new life chapter, we feel sad and empty. Leaving Ibanda was painful and would have been unbearable had Rwanzo not been by our side as we drove away from the village. Certainly our unknown destination and lack of career plan make dog-ownership difficult at this point, but sometimes the easy way is not the best way. After hurdling several complications, we put Rwanzo on an airplane and sent him to Arizona. There he will stay with Bob's high school buddy Mike for three months, as we travel.

As you know from your visit in Ibanda, we agonized for months over the decision to bring Rwanzo with us to the States. Bringing an African dog into the US is costly and can involve obstacles through customs. However, unlike European countries, who impose long quarantines, the USA simply requires a thorough examination and a number of inoculations.

In a very heartfelt letter, Bob's dad explained the challenges we would face importing an African dog to the US. He knew from his visit here that Rwanzo is quite a handful. His letter was sensible, yet sensitive to our love for our dog. But, essentially, he said, "Don't bring the dog home."

This was very difficult counsel for Bob to accept from his dad. And certainly, it meant that we couldn't ask Bob's parents to keep Rwanzo while we travel! I don't know how we thought of Mike, but Bob figured his buddy owed him a few favors from bailouts during their youth. In a phone call from Kampala, Mike gladly accepted the responsibility, saying, "Send him on!"

Perhaps the most phenomenal part of the story about sending Rwanzo home was the supernatural influence which solidified Bob's decision. Even after Mike had agreed to keep Rwanzo for several months, we still struggled with the decision. The travel, the health considerations, and our undetermined future — my father-in-law's words rung true and clear. It was not practical. Two things occurred that helped us make the decision about bringing Rwanzo home.

We received a three-month-old letter from Habitat, notifying us of a stipend increase that gave us exactly the amount of money needed to send Rwanzo home. That solved the financial challenge; however, up until one week before our departure, we were still undecided.

As we went to bed one night, I said to Bob, "This is your decision. I will support you either way. We have prayed about this for months. It's time to make the decision and do what is necessary in carrying out the decision we make."

Bob responded with melancholy, "I'm going to sleep on it one more night."

The next morning a familiar hum woke us. Poking his head through the slit in the mosquito net on Bob's side of the bed was Rwanzo, looking for Bob's attention. This was not Rwanzo's usual morning greeting; he often started at the window, barking at the chickens and goats who are the first to rattle the stillness of daybreak. This morning was different. He stood by the edge of the bed with his chin resting on Bob's chest. I cuddled Bob from the other side, resting my head upon his shoulder. As if saying the "Amen" of a prayer, Bob blurted out, "We're taking him!"

"Are you sure? Will you be at peace with that decision, even when complications arise?"

"Absolutely, this is the only choice for us."

I quickly responded, "Well, let's get moving. We'll have to fetch Nyasyo to build a travel crate."

Excited about his decision, Bob hopped out of bed and said, "I'll ride my bike up to Nyasyo's house and on the way back, I'll start collecting whatever building materials we need for the crate.

As Bob was pulling on his trousers, I looked out our front window and was shocked to see Nyasyo standing by our fence.

"Bob, Nyasyo is here!"

Bob hustled to the fence to greet Nyasyo. "*Kuti Bwa. Wa henoende?*" (Hello my friend, how are you?)

"*Ah Yi, Aneyo Ndeke.*" (Everything is okay)

"I was coming to see you today. We need your help."

"I know. That's why I'm here."

Nyasyo wore a tape measure around his neck and he had a pencil tucked behind his ear. He was ready to measure Rwanzo and study the cage specifications provided by British Airways.

After Bob regained his composure from the shock of Nyasyo's unexpected appearance at our house, (we hadn't seen Nyasyo for weeks) he asked, "Can you build this cage within a couple of days? We leave on Tuesday."

"I can."

Bob came back into the house and found me in the kitchen where I had overheard the whole conversation through the open window. He then hugged me so hard that I thought my ribs would crack. Bob had been affirmed through "an angel" (as we later referred to Nyasyo) that the very difficult decision he made was the right decision. With his hug, he squeezed out the last bit of tension that had built up in him (and in me) and never looked back on his decision.

Now Rwanzo is enjoying the luxuries of the US, lying on carpet and swimming in a pool with Mike's dog, Sparky. Just before we boarded a bus to Tanzania, we received a fax from Mike, stating that he had successfully retrieved Rwanzo from the Phoenix Airport. Rwanzo made the two-day, three-connection flight, all by himself!

Not seamlessly however. We had to sedate him heavily in order to crate him for the duration of the travel; I was worried about effects the medication would have on him. And, his handmade wooden crate did not pass code in London. Thankfully, they swapped his cage for another one in the London airport and got him on a connecting flight to the US. Amazingly, Rwanzo's flight arrived one hour before a major earthquake jolted LA, and he was transferred successfully on to his last flight, which landed in Phoenix.

After wrangling with a customer service rep over the $250 crate charges, Mike cleared Rwanzo's airport departure and drove him to his home in Tempe.

Besides a little culture shock: barking at his reflection in the mirror and at the TV (both of which he has never seen), it sounds like Rwanzo is healthy and happy. We can't wait to reunite with him in a few months. We also look forward to seeing family and friends. Perhaps the travel time will blur the goodbyes while building excitement for reconnecting with folks back home. We also hope to gain insight about what's next for us: Graduate school? Jobs? Where to live? Our future is open-ended.

See you soon,
Carrie

How could a pressure lamp, a gas oven, and a dog make such a drastic difference in our happiness? Well, the truth is, that those things, in and of themselves, did not transform our lives. Collectively, they represent a time when our spirits had been transformed. We regained our inner peace and renewed our ability to appreciate simple pleasures. We did not do this on our own; rather, we had been given the peace that passes understanding. Of course, there are numerous interpretations and commentaries on this popular biblical passage. My pastor described it beautifully when he talked about a peace within the midst of trouble – feeling calm when surrounded by madness. While I agree that the peace can be an inner serenity surrounded by an external conflict, I also believe that it can be the stillness before or following a storm. Either way, the peace that passes understanding is a gift from God, another aspect of His grace: undeserved and freely given.

As we left Uganda, we gave the lamp and the oven to others who would appreciate the joys of simple luxuries. The stories of Rwanzo continued for another ten years, creating memories for many people around the world, as we continued working internationally with Habitat, and later settling in the mountains of North Carolina. Bob's dad became great friends with Rwanzo and the disagreement about bringing the dog home became just another story for us to laugh about. The next time we came home from Africa with Rwanzo, following our three years in South Africa, Bob's parents collected Rwanzo from the airport after his 20 hour flight and fed him three Wendy's hamburgers.

The lamp, the oven, and the dog: each holds its story, but most of all, they symbolize a time of peace. They represent the calm after a storm and they mark a time in our marriage when the anonymous prayer at our wedding was most fulfilled: "I wish you love and strength and wisdom, and gold enough to help some needy one. I wish you song but also blessed silence and God's sweet peace when every day is done."

The peace that passes understanding is God's sweet peace and it is given to us when we have followed our hearts: when we have prayerfully made a decision – one that may oppose common sense yet feels right. That peace allows us to move forward without regrets, having faith that we have made the right decisions.

Bob's "Ode to Rwanzo," written in November 2004, a week after we buried our beloved dog in our backyard.

Ode to Rwanzo
August 12, 1992 – September 12, 2004

I feel as though I have a hole in my gut. My shoulders are slumped. My head is heavy. My heart aches. A sea of sadness stirs inside me and I can feel the tears well up in my eyes. Depending upon where I am, I either let the tears flow or I try to suppress them. Emptiness. Melancholy. Aching.

My dog, my trusted friend, my confidant. He's not wagging his tail, running up to the car when I come home from work, nor the first to greet me. I look for him when I get out of bed in the middle of the night, to avoid stepping on him. He's not there. Nor is he lying under the dining room table at dinner.

Rwanzo offered comfort and compassion and also wildness and energy. He could run like the wind, grab my shoe in full stride and trip me. Then he would stand over me – the victorious warrior. Nobility ran in his blood as he guarded the yard and protected his family: head high and chest out. He was strong and powerful, yet graceful. He was to be admired, and feared, by those who did not know him. A pure blooded Rwenzori Ridgeback I used to call him; he was unique to the world.

He was not a perfect dog, but our Rwanzo was an excellent dog. He had a mischievous side. He would play as hard as you wanted, sometimes biting down on your arm until it hurt, but never bled. He could be rough, and gentle, yet always playful. He and I learned to communicate quite well. He knew me and I knew him. Had he been a person, he would have been a noble leader. He would have been a sinner, but chased after God's embrace. And while he was "bad" sometimes, he had a heart of gold.

For a month, Rwanzo was ill. The vet could not find anything wrong. But since he was 12 years old we knew the end could be near. On Sunday he lost all strength to stand. In the evening I carried him to our bedroom where he had been sleeping since his health began to decline. After putting the kids to bed, I came to be with him, to rub his soft fur, especially his ears, his paws, and his head.

I came to comfort him. For a month he had been fighting whatever sickness was eating at him. He was tired. He couldn't wag his tail. Only his eyes, his expressive eyes, could speak. As I rubbed his head that night, I whispered in his ear, "Its okay. You've carried us for 12 years through difficult and good times – through four moves, three countries, several years without kids and several years as our boys' best friend. This is your time. If you need to go, you can go."

His eyes studied me. I yelled for Carrie to come in and join me. Then, he stretched back and took four more breaths. I held his head. Carrie held his chest and felt his last heartbeat. And we loved him as he went on to be with his Maker.

Thank you God, for sharing Rwanzo with us. I do believe you sent him to us, that you lived in him, and taught and comforted us through him. He was family, with us every step of the way. If I can get my arms around "heaven," I know that Rwanzo will be amongst the first to greet me there, running up to me, tail wagging, ears raised, eyes focused, barking "Catch me if you dare!" My broken heart will hopefully heal and I will be able to get on with life. Yet I know, the memory of Rwanzo will live on in me, and those he touched, forever and ever and ever.

Bob

Seasons

As annual seasons circle our lives and shape our activities, we slowly grow into maturity and wisdom. Likewise, life seasons, though not contained in a time frame, present the changes, challenges and nourishment that are necessary for growth. Without a change in seasons, we would become stagnant, stale or complacent. Let us welcome the "time for everything" and seek the knowledge that is encapsulated in the seeds planted. Let us also be patient with the circle of life, appreciating the newness that each rotation brings.

I end the Epiphany Chapters with this one on seasons as I am ending a life season and beginning a new one. This season, or life chapter, which has spanned three years, has mirrored the emotional and spiritual stages of personal development that painted my three-year term in Uganda. If I were to depict the past three years of writing this book, you would see similar highs and lows, a continual wrestle with truth, and ultimately a re-submission to a higher power. The current change of seasons, marked by making a return trip to Uganda, is blanketed with the peace that passes understanding. This peace results from the transformation of my fears to faith, my guilt to gratitude and God's vision to His provision.

> *There is a time for everything, and a season for every activity under heaven: a time to be born and a time to die, a time to plant and a time to uproot, a time to kill and a time to heal, a time to tear down and a time to build, a time to weep and a time to laugh, a time to mourn and a time to dance, a time to scatter stones and a time to gather them, a time to embrace and a time to refrain, a time to search and a time to give up, a time to keep and a time to throw away, a time to tear and a time to mend, a time to be silent and a time to speak, a time to love and a time to hate, a time for war and a time for peace.*
>
> *Ecclesiastes 3:1-8*

April 1993
Dear Bonnie,

We were walking home from a family selection visit when the sky opened and dumped its daily downpour. What had been a hot, blue-sky day was quickly overtaken by a rush of billowing clouds. The transition from sunshine to sheets of rain happened within a matter of minutes.

Still an hour's walk from home, we ducked under the overhang of the nearest home. There were five of us: three family selection committee members in addition to Bob and me. Nelson, Betty and Peredasi often make these selection visits, which are the basis for choosing families who will receive Habitat assistance on their houses.

We stood under the rusty tin roof of a mud house. The 18-inch overhang barely covered our heads. The splatter of rain from the muddy ground bounced back to our sandaled feet. Other people joined us, taking refuge from the driving rain. All villagers scrambled to seek cover, if only under a banana tree. While we were carrying only a daypack, others were hauling goats and produce – some had bikes. It didn't take long for people to settle into hideouts. A few women came out of their homes to place red and green basins on their verandas; every drop of water collected is one less to carry from the river.

The raindrops came hard and fast, unlike the gentle shower we had yesterday. The pitter patter on the roof top was loud enough to discourage any conversation. We stood in silence. As if listening to a choir in a worship service, we gave reverence to the creator who gives rain.

When the cascade had slowed to a trickle, Nelson said, "Let's walk. The rains have finished." He knows the rain patterns well. Within ten steps of our journey home, the sky had returned to solid blue and people were back to their *shambas*, (gardens)carrying on with work as if there had been no interruption. Our clothes, which were wet but not drenched, nearly dried by the time we got home.

All was well at our house. We had remembered to close our window shutters. However, we had forgotten to bring our laundry inside from our clothes line. Now, for the third day in a row, we are draping the same trousers, t-shirts and skirts over our chair backs in the house. I think we shall become better planners and arrange for someone to collect our clothes before the showers when we are away for the whole day.

It is rainy season! And, similar to the host of seasonal activities ushered in by summer, fall, winter, and spring, rainy season here shapes peoples' days quite differently than does the dry season.

It all begins with the swarming of termites. For months during the dry season, termites build their mud mountains; some are four feet high! One of the funniest sights is a goat perched on top of a termite mound, his feet balanced on the peak, which is only a foot in diameter. I wonder why goats do this?!? Just knowing that the inside of these mounds is crawling with tunnels of termites gives me the heebie jeebies.

Just after the first rain, termites come out of their mounds by the thousands and take flight. Ugandans collect the termites, some while in flight, but mostly those that have landed on the ground. First peeling off the wings, people either eat the fresh termite bodies or gather them for making termite paste. Termite paste, made by pounding the termites, is a seasonal delicacy enjoyed by people across the continent. I have tried goat's stomach and other unrecognizable meat innards, but I can't seem to get termite paste past my lips.

Rainy season alters villagers' work. Building and brick making have slowed to nearly a halt. While the rain is not constant, it is daily, usually a storm in the morning and late afternoon. Those things dependent upon sun to dry – cement, clay, laundry – don't get enough dry air. So building is typically a dry season activity. This frustrated us at first, but we now use the time during rainy season for homeowner education and project planning.

The farmers in western Uganda (which includes most of the population) are busy preparing their soil and sowing seeds. As if a weight has been lifted from their shoulders, people move about with cheerfulness as they hoe their land and plant their gardens. Perhaps the change of season offers a fresh start, new life and hope for bountiful harvest. While the two main staple foods, banana trees and cassava root, grow year-round, potatoes, groundnuts, corn and tomatoes are planted in the rainy season.

For me, the first drops of rain here are like the first green sprouts to pop through the hard winter's ground back home. The promise of spring uplifts my spirits and reminds me of how powerful and gracious our creator is. And while I appreciate the change of season here, I do miss spring in North Carolina. I miss the early crocuses and daffodils that blossom in spite of the lingering chill. They are God's messengers telling us that we have nearly made it through winter. Soon thereafter, a symphony of color fills the neighborhood. Pink cherry blossoms and white dogwood flowers sing in harmonious undertones, while brilliant yellow forsythia shouts interludes of sopranic joy. I smile as I close my eyes and imagine the show. Purple and yellow irises pipe in near the end of the piece with a repetitive rhythm that carries into the warmer temperatures of summer. That's the beauty of the mind; it can take you anywhere you want to go.

I am also thankful for the rainy season here in Uganda. We have planted our carrots, squash and okra – produce they do not sell in the markets. The midday rains give us an excuse to close our doors and windows and tune out all but the chorus of raindrops beating on our tin roof. Bob and I sometimes play cards, and oftentimes we escape into a good novel. The simplicity of life without electricity has become a valued asset that I hope we never forget how to enjoy. I think of the busy lifestyles in America and I am repulsed by the thought of the whirlwind of activities and expectations that prevent us from pausing to enjoy the splendor of a good rain.

I wish you a beautiful spring.

Love,
Carrie

Journal Entry
November 1992

Three people have drowned in the Mobuku River this season. The Mobuku River runs through the valley of Bugoye sub county, dividing Ibanda from Kyanya and many other villages that make up our project area. People cross the river regularly for normal activities such as going to school, walking to the market or doing business. There is a footbridge two kilometers from our home in the Ibanda trading center, but that bridge is a bit far for people who live higher in the mountains. Therefore, they cross the river in various spots closer to their homes. Some river crossing spots host large boulders while others have fallen logs that serve as a bridge. Whatever the case, these crossing methods become challenging and risky during the high water levels accumulated during the rainy season. It can be hazardous and perilous, since the Bakonzo people generally cannot swim.

I did not know two of the people who lost their lives this year, but I did know one. He was a village elder, a well respected man of many years.

Job keeps talking about building a bridge that would connect Ibanda trading center to Kyanya trading center (where he lives). "We are only lacking funds," he says. I hope and pray that his dream of building a bridge becomes a reality one day.

Unlike the locals' quandary, the river poses no real threat to me and Bob during the rainy season because we usually choose to walk the extra distance to the footbridge. And if we do decide to cross using stones, we are confident that our swimming skills would save us in the unlikely event of slipping and getting swept away by the river.

If we are headed north on the Kyanya side of the river, the extended walk can add an hour to our journey; but part of the fun is the journey. We enjoy encountering people along the way and witnessing life through their maze of daily activities. We are usually not in a hurry to get anywhere, as rushing from here to there is counter-culture. I carry my produce basket because we often meet someone selling tomatoes, mangoes or peanuts along the way. Occasionally, we stop to buy *cavalagala*, banana pancakes that are deep-fried in palm oil.

SAD NEWS IN THE AREA
We lost a woman on 27th August, river accident (drown) she was a daughter of the widow - Elivaniya Kitsa, Habitat home owner, she was married in the clan of Daneri Irumba at Nyakisabu Kyanya village near my home.

We spent 5 five days looking for the dead body which we found on the 6th day at Bugoye area.

My struggle with the rainy season is towards the end of it when I'm frustrated with muddy roads and laundry that seems to never completely dry. Yesterday Bob and I went to Kitswamba, a village just over the mountain from us. Kitswamba is within the Rwenzori Habitat project area and Bob and I are responsible for occasionally checking in on the project committee.

Only a few kilometers as a crow flies, Kitswamba is beyond walking distance because of the steep terrain. We drove our *picky picky* (motorbike) down the valley and for a short bit on the main tarmac road, then back up another dirt road to the Kitswamba trading center. This u-shaped journey usually takes an hour. But of course, on our way, the clouds rolled in and released themselves. What is often a welcome break in the day was a great hindrance. We had to stop and wait out the rain, causing us to take two hours to arrive at our destination. The Habitat meeting we went to attend was cancelled because there was not a quorum; only three of the nine committee members turned up. Our long, muddy ride to Kitswamba was not only a waste of our day, but was even more elongated by the failure of our picky picky on the way home. We had made it as far as Maliba before the bike chain came off. Bob's attempt to repair the motorbike was unsuccessful and had we not encountered a few willing children to help us push the bike across the footbridge and up Ibanda road, we would have arrived home long after dark.

All this – to go three kilometers to a meeting that didn't happen.

I am ready for a change of seasons. I feel waterlogged. I need sunshine and dry air. I have popped three mango worms out of Bob's back in the past couple of weeks. These worms are a result of eggs laid in our clothing by mango flies. When our clothes on the line do not fully dry, the miniscule eggs get into our skin where they hatch and grow into worms. If I was better about ironing our clothes, we could prevent the mango worms. However, it's such an ordeal to fire up coals to put in the iron, that I mostly skip this activity.

Probably more frustrating than the mango worms is the dampness of our bed sheets. They are not wet, but they feel moist. Oh, how I long for sheets and towels just out of the dryer with that fresh Downy fragrance!

Rainy season has fashioned some funny stories, like the time Bob began "singing in the rain" while riding on the back of a pickup truck with lots of Ugandan passengers. We were on our way to visit friends up in Kilembe. They have electricity and a TV. We were headed to watch a six-month-old video tape of the Washington Redskins winning the Super Bowl.

Chock full of people, the vehicle swayed as we stood huddled together, arms linked to hold everyone in. Then, the rains came. Raindrops hit harder on moving targets; we were getting pelted. From behind, I imagine the truckload looked like a football team, circling up for the "break."

Perhaps Bob needed a release or wanted to add more excitement to the trip when he belted out, a little left of in tune, "Hail to the Redskins…" Certainly I was the only one who knew what Redskins are or even understood what Bob was singing, so the locals followed my lead in laughter at Bob's joyous chant. Soon, we were all laughing and singing in the rain. I often wonder how these stories come across at their dinner tables. I'm sure they shared a good laugh with their families about the crazy mzungu singing on public transport.

January 1994
Dear Mom and Dad,

I can't believe we are leaving Ibanda next month. Another life season is nearing its end and once again I am teetering between highs and lows. Some days I feel ready to go, as I think ahead to being with family and enjoying all the comforts of stateside living. I can almost taste the pizza, Raisin Bran® with **cold** milk and mint chocolate chip ice-cream. But when I think of saying goodbyes to our Ugandan friends, I feel sick to my stomach. In many ways, leaving here feels as traumatic as leaving Charlotte did three years ago. I'll never forget driving down your driveway for the last time, our car packed with the four bags we would take on the airplane to Africa. We had given our last bear hugs and shed an ocean of tears. I closed my door and rolled down my window.

As Bob released the car breaks and the car began coasting down the drive, Mandy walked alongside my car door, clutching the door jamb as if she couldn't let it go. I was afraid to look up at my sister's face. Seeing her pain would cause me to burst into tears all over again. Instead of looking at her, I placed my hand on top of hers to express one last time how much I love her. I wish that I had left it at that, but I caught one last glimpse of her in my side-view mirror. Her horrified expression showed that she was afraid this could be the last time we would ever see each other. I felt doubt and regret about our decision to be far away from home for three years.

I feel a similar pain now; only this time I feel more certain that I will never see these friends again. While Ibanda is not a replacement for what I call "home," it has been our home and we have grown to cherish people here like family.

The uncertainty of what we will do and where we will live when we get back to the States ramps up our anxiety all the more. We look forward to our time of extensive travel after we leave here. We are hopeful that God will direct our path for our next life's season.

We have missed you and the family and we anxiously anticipate our reunion with you. Your visit here meant the world to us and your familiarity with village life will make it much easier to share our experiences with you. I have no idea how we will share Uganda's dichotomy of simplicity and complexity with folks back home.

You remember Job who gave you a tour of the Habitat office? He and other Habitat committee members are afraid that this project will fall apart when Bob and I leave. We have done our best to work ourselves out of a job. We have trained staff, committee members and homeowners. They do everything. We have been their cheerleaders over the past three months, refusing to do any project tasks. We feel that they are capable and have the integrity necessary for making Habitat sustainable here.

But they will have to withstand critique for countering the more common model of project operations. Typically villagers rely on outside money and leadership for development. Unfortunately, top-down development dominates the country, perhaps because most people (including donors) do not have the patience or understanding of the time investment necessary for true sustainable community development.

As we prepare to leave Ibanda, we celebrate the friendships we have made and the success of the Habitat project. Over 75 houses scattered through the foothills of the Rwenzori Mountains shimmer as they reflect the sun on their new Habitat tin roofs. Homeowners have worked in small groups and are holding each other accountable for making their house payments. The style of micro-credit financing, which we modeled after the Grameen Bank in Bangladesh, has worked well in this community. Bob's communication with the founder and director of Grameen Bank, Muhammad Yunus, was worth the effort! We were shocked to receive educational materials from Yunus after sending him a handwritten letter from Uganda to Bangladesh!

Our conviction to establish a sustainable house building program in Uganda, contrary to Habitat's traditional model, though nearly getting us fired, was the right thing to do. We are ever thankful to have been given the opportunity to develop this project using methodologies that we believe in.

GRAMEEN BANK

With the best compliments of

Professor Muhammad Yunus
Managing Director

Mirpur-2, Dhaka-1216, Bangladesh.
Phone:-801138/803559(Off) 801247(Res)
Fax No:-880-2-803559

We leave the Habitat project in good hands and we feel grateful that it has brought people together to address the common need of simple, decent and affordable housing. We celebrate people who have shared in the vision, put forth their time and effort, and have contributed to making a difference in their own community.

I do not want to say goodbye to these friends. Especially Job. There's just something about Job.

Love,
Carrie

WINTER 1994

UGANDA HABITAT FOR HUMANITY

the. Wazunguwitness

NEWS FROM RWENZORI HABITAT FOR HUMANITY

Uganda Habitat National and International Partners at National Partners training

Bob & Carrie Wagner
Rwenzori
Habitat for Humanity
Post Office Box 46
Kasese, Uganda
East Africa

Wazungu (Wä - zoon - gu) noun: A friendly term East Africans use for "white people."

Thank you for your prayers, letters and financial support that make our work possible.

Thanks to Steven Huff (919-724-0643) for the design and layout of our newsletters, Byron Baldwin for handling our black & white film, and to Anne & Mark Tiberio (704-347-5760) for coordinating the mailings.

Tax deductable donations can be sent to Habitat for Humanity International, 121 Habitat St., Americus, GA, 31709. Please indicate on your check: Wagner-02714. Thank You.

Please contact Anne Tiberio (704-347-5760) for address changes at 2001 Chambwood Drive, Charlotte, NC, 28205.

Farewell to Uganda

This morning I took a long walk on the beach. Endless palm trees on my left and vast blue ocean on my right. In front of me and behind me, nothing but a strong seaborn breeze. What a liberating feeling to see only my footprints in the sand for a stretch of a kilometer. We are on vacation in Zanzibar, or maybe I should say a "sabbatical." We have finished our term with Habitat for Humanity and are taking a few months to travel on our way home. This journey will slowly take us from the Third world to the First world via Africa, Indonesia, New Zealand, Fiji and across the United States.

The past two months have been filled with tying loose ends, packing and saying farewells. It is only now (ten days out of Uganda) that I am able to think clearly and differentiate the various feelings I have.

> 66
> Leaving Ibanda was more difficult than we had imagined.
> 99

Leaving Ibanda was more difficult than we had imagined. For several months, we prepared mentally for the big change we had coming; fin-

ishing our three year term, going back to the States, and leaving behind a different world and life style. We were a little less prepared for the actual "goodbyes."

I remember leaving home in June 1991, anticipating Africa, yet clinging on to last moments with family and friends. Those farewells were hard, but I knew they were all only temporary, and that if necessary, I could return. The farewells in Uganda were different – leaving a place and people we love, knowing that we may never see them again.

December and January provided a mixed bag of both hecticness and fun. Projectwise, it was one of our busiest times as we and our committee were trying to squeeze in as much as possible before we left.

Christmas was simple and quiet. We attended a Christmas Eve communion service and enjoyed the usual beating of drums and Bakonjo singing. It did not, however, feel like Christmas. So after the service, the expatriates from our village (three European Catholic sisters, two Zairean sisters, two Peace Corps volunteers and ourselves) gathered outside the church to sing Silent Night.

There is always sadness and joy wrapped up in the change of seasons. Anticipation, excitement and hope are tempered by melancholy, insecurity, and loss. As I finish packing for our return trip to Uganda and write this last Epiphany chapter, I am once again changing seasons. What began with a divine vision three years ago and has been a provisional search ever since, has come to an end, and I am completely blown away at how God has orchestrated the chain of events.

This season began in February, 2006 with a vision. I journaled about the vision two years later in order to remain focused and faithful in my search for clarity. Recording the vision experience recaptured the magic for me and gave me a platform from which to share the spiritual nature of the book and return trip to Uganda.

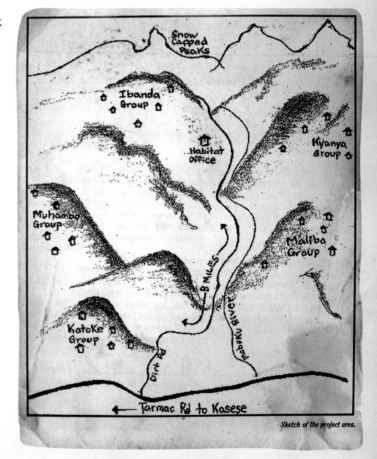

Sketch of the project area.

Journal Entry
March 25, 2008

I was determined to conquer seasonal depression that winter. Part of my strategy was to hike, even on cold mornings that tempted me to stay in, buckle down to my computer and work. Sally was a good motivator; she didn't care about the cold. She so longed for adventure and the chance to sniff out all the smells of Butler Mountain. In the mornings, Sally spent half an hour in our own yard, snorting and barking while I cleaned the kitchen and did my usual morning routine.

When Sally came in, she would tell me very politely with her bright green eyes, "Put on your walking shoes, Mom – it's time to go up the mountain." So we did, often three times a week.

Sally and I walked up the road that winds its way to the top of our mountain, past neighborhood houses that have great views of Asheville's surrounding mountains. Beyond the houses, I could let Sally off leash and continue up a very steep, dirt road that zigzags about a half mile further up the mountain. Where the road stops is where we always stopped and turned around to go home.

Until one day.

We stopped and stood there for a minute, wondering what's at the top of Butler Mountain and why am I so compelled to go up there?

I prayed for guidance and safety and turned to Sally, who had already started back down the mountain, and said, "Come on girl! Let's go!" Sally was at my feet in a flash and soon was forging a trail through the unknown territory. Typical Beagle style, nose to the ground, she scooted through trees and vines, wagging her tail in delight at the stories told by the fragrances of the forest.

I followed Sally, crunching the winter leaves beneath my feet. I didn't fear getting lost because we were headed straight up and I knew that home was straight down.

The experience in store for me was the beginning of what would become a new chapter in my spiritual journey.

We had bushwhacked no more than a quarter of a mile when the forest opened up and gave way to a break in the tree line; yet it wasn't the top of the mountain.

I could still see the top beyond the break. As I hoisted myself over a couple of boulders and pulled through the trees, I found myself standing on a road. A ROAD circles the top of Butler Mountain! I'm sure lots of people know about this road, which is an access road for the gated community on the other side of the mountain, but I certainly did not!

I could see for miles in both directions. My heart raced. Sally and I swiftly walked the entire road that circles the mountain, eventually finding a small footpath that leads to the very top.

The top of Butler is a flat bald, about the size of a football field. It's the kind of space that begs for running, lying down to look at the expansive sky or just breathing in the views. Sally and I did all three.

After taking it all in, we began our descent, making one more loop around the summit road. It was on this last loop that the most extraordinary thing happened to me. Since that moment I have called it a "vision." But thinking back, it began with a supernatural whisper that permeated my body. "God, is that you?" I asked. I felt as if God was using the Holy Spirit to get my attention, in order to prepare me for the ideas that He would flood into my heart and mind. So surreal was this feeling that I cannot put it into words.

I "saw" a book filled with the faces of Uganda, people who had so challenged yet enriched my spiritual journey. I saw their simple, yet complex way of life. I saw children who would have grown up now, and wondered what kind of path they had taken, what, if any, opportunities had come their way. And I saw Job Malighee, the man who had most influenced my three years living in Uganda, and whose village wisdom set examples that would impact our lives forever.

As I thought about these people, this culture in a land far away, impoverished financially, yet rich in many other ways, I heard God saying, "Share their story. Share your story."

When I had the vision for this book, I had no idea that 65,000 words would emerge. Finding the words to express my epiphanies has made the past three years an inward journey. I have immersed myself into Uganda once again, reading and rewriting journal entries and personal letters. Through my writing I have traveled and settled into the village that transformed me.

This season of travel could be called a rainy season because of the constant showers of blessings. God has opened doors and guided my steps, affirming my decisions along the way. However, the past three years have also seen long, dry, thirsty days. There have been dark, cold stretches too. It has been a season to remember, a season of transformation. I guess God is not finished with us until He's done.

I knew that completing this story would involve a return trip to Uganda. I had to rely on God's provision for that endeavor as well. Planning the trip, raising the funds and preparing our children for third world travel has been a faith walk in itself. And I'm sure that God has another set of lessons for me, Bob and our children embedded in the trip that lies ahead.

Uganda Revisited

Mission trip. Purposeful travel. Ecotour.
We go with the intent to serve, learn and grow.
Though we have planned an itinerary, we are open to detours, setbacks
and new directions. We anticipate surprises and look forward to divine
connections. We take each step in faith that God will provide, protect
and forgive. We go and do, but mostly we go and be. For it is being present,
taking part in people's lives, that transforms us all.

"Passengers, please take your seats, buckle your seatbelts and prepare for departure. British Airways flight number 63 from London Heathrow to Entebbe, Uganda will be lifting momentarily. Please enjoy your flight."

I pinched myself to determine whether this was another one of my dreams or if I was actually sitting on a plane beside my delightful sons, Adam and Benjamin, and my wonderful husband, Bob.

Anticipation. Amazement. Wonder. Few concerns, but some. I had prepared my spirit, mind and body for this heartening and physically challenging adventure. I was ready, but still in disbelief that it was truly happening. We had raised $17,000 for our mission trip. Over 300 people were supporting us, financially and prayerfully. These friends would be eager to hear our stories upon our return.

I had finally surrendered to God's timing and was relishing in the splendor of seeing His plan unfold. My contrived plan for the return to Uganda had expired long ago. In retrospect, my sketchy outline paled in comparison to the organic flow of connections that had transpired over the past two years. Only a divine master could orchestrate such a plan.

As I closed my eyes, silently praying for safe travel, I heard the words spoken to me by my dear friend Elaine, "God will give the provision when the vision is clear." These are words I have clung to since March of 2008, when she prayed for me "that fears and doubts would succumb to faith." Among several other close friends, Elaine had journeyed with me through three years since the vision: through doubt, faith, listening, discernment and receiving God's grace. She was certainly with me in spirit on this trip, even though she couldn't physically be here.

Several others were with me in spirit: certainly Frye Gaillard. Although I was not yet at peace with the abrupt cancellation of his and his wife Nancy's trip (due to illness), by this point I had learned to let go of things beyond my control. Frye was to be the co-author of this book and would have been the main journalist for the trip. I mostly felt sad for the overwhelming disappointment that the Gaillards must have experienced.

They too had gotten a multitude of shots and invested lots of time and money, anticipating what could have been a trip of a lifetime. And though deep in my gut I knew that I now carried full responsibility for writing the book, I was able to suppress that anxiety with the excitement for all that awaited us.

"Mom. Mom. We need to take our malaria pills." My silence was broken by Adam. I opened my eyes to my beautiful 12-year-old, whose soft blue eyes radiated anticipation and excitement. I looked beyond him to Benjamin, Adam's little brother and my "little Boo." Benjamin already had headphones hugging his ears and was happily studying the *In-Flight* entertainment guide.

For a split second, I thought about the health risks in taking our children to a developing country: the potential for illness, accidents, even tragedies that occur more frequently than in our first world country. My faith quickly squashed my fears and I was able to respond with a smile, "Thanks for remembering the pills, Adam. Can you believe we are halfway to Africa?"

"Uganda, here we come!" Adam exclaimed, smiling and banging his hands down on the arm rests. Three movies later, we arrived in Entebbe. As Benjamin wrote in his journal, *"When I woke up, I was in Uganda. I looked out the window of the plane and saw trees that were flat on top."*

Our first week in Uganda was invaluable. Spending a few days in the capital city of Kampala and a few days on the road to visit various missionaries and development projects gave us ample time to adjust our internal clocks, while dipping our toes into Ugandan culture. Bob's and my reentry to Uganda was our kid's entry, and though he and I needed a little time to ease back into familiarity, we were most interested in moving at an appropriate pace for our children. Making time to share and have them reflect on observations and perceptions was of utmost importance. We designed this trip around Adam and Benjamin; they were not "tag- alongs" to adult-focused mission activities.

We had planned to stay in Ibanda, where we would engage in a community-based soccer program and visit schools. We had brought with us 150 student-written books from Adam and Benjamin's schools. These very personal and precious books would be given to students in the village schools. We also brought 12 bags of donated soccer equipment to be used by Community Development through Sport (CDTS), a grassroots organization that serves 12,000 Ugandan kids through soccer and netball. It took over a year to establish contact and nurture these connections, but the relational aspect of our trip was truly the core of the mission. We knew that the real value of this month-long journey would be nestled in our relationships with people.

"Are you okay with me taking the boys on a walk through the city?" asked Stephen. "Um. . . Sure," I responded to the man we had met just yesterday upon our arrival in the airport. After all, another principle of our trip was about trust, letting go, and nurturing cross-cultural relationships, so I figured I would set that tone right from the start. Off Adam and Benjamin went into the hustle and bustle of one of the busiest African cities – with practically a stranger.

We had been emailing Stephen for months, learning about his work in Ibanda and surrounding villages. In fact, CDTS, initiated by Stephen, was the very hook that lured Bob into the return trip to Uganda.

Through three cell phone calls, a few text messages and several emails, Bob and Stephen began a friendship based on mutual interest in village level soccer in the Rwenzori Mountains. The only thing we knew about Stephen before meeting him in Uganda (besides his involvement with the soccer program) was that he was from Scotland and had lived in Ibanda for two years.

That had been enough information for us. With enthusiasm and promotion for the sports program, our family with the help of some church friends, collected a garage full of used and new soccer equipment from our local soccer families. We also sent $1,000 prior to our trip to sponsor some of the program needs of CDTS. Though we did not know Stephen, we knew the tremendous need in Ibanda and we were thrilled to have an opportunity to engage our local community in providing tangible support for Ugandan kids.

Stephen didn't know much about the Wagners either, except for the fact that he had already received money through Western Union from us (which he was thrilled with) and that we would be bringing loads of cleats, shin guards, uniforms and soccer balls for his program. He also knew that we were looking for a fantastic, yet authentic village experience for our kids: an opportunity he took ownership for and looked forward to providing. He later told us that he suspected we were a little unique in our choosing Ibanda over Disney World for a family holiday.

Two adults and two kids pushing four carts toppling over with 16 bags (4 backpacks and 12 huge duffle bags), the Wagners were easy to spot coming out of the airport.

"Carrie. Are you Carrie?" I looked at the only man waiting outside of the customs exit door. He looked nothing like the Stephen I was expecting. My first thought was that perhaps he is Stephen's driver. Then, pointing to his chest, he spread a smile of nicotine stained teeth, minus one up front, and said, "Stephen."

His black skull cap, ragged teeth and sleeveless t-shirt gave him the appearance of a pirate. He was not the tall, pale-skinned Scotsman I had expected.

"Oh, nice to meet you," I responded, trying to conceal my surprise. "These are our soccer players, Adam and Benjamin." Adam and Benjamin stepped forward and shook Stephen's hand with timidity but politeness. Thankfully, Bob broke the awkwardness with an enthusiastic, "Stephen! Finally. We're so glad to meet you." Bob and Stephen hugged as if they were old friends.

Secretly, I was intrigued that one of our two main hosts in Uganda looked contrary to how we had envisioned him. I knew that he must have quite a life story and I looked forward to breaking through stereotypes and judgments to learn who Stephen really is and why God had sent him to Uganda.

Into a van we piled: the four Wagners, Stephen, his Ugandan friend Samuel, a driver and 16 bags. Benjamin sat on Samuel's lap and Stephen and I propped ourselves on a pile of duffle bags. On the ride into the city, Stephen was quick to explain his heritage. Half American Indian and half Pakistani, at two months old Stephen was adopted by Scottish parents and had grown up in the UK. That explained his complexion. The rest of his story we would learn later – and what a story it is! (I will tell you more about his story in the Afterword.)

Stephen took us to our hotel in Kampala where we would stay three nights. He then traveled the eight hour drive to Ibanda, on his own with the donated equipment. We stayed in Kampala to buy supplies for our long journey.

I sat by an open window at the bar on the 4th floor of the Aponye Hotel in Kampala, sipping my *Kress* Bitter Lemon while waiting for Mugisha, our friend and former neighbor from Ibanda. (Bob and the boys were sorting through our bags in a storage room.) The street life below looked surprisingly the same as it did when we left Uganda in 1994, although it appeared busier: more vibrant with activity and traffic. Most of the pedal bikes have been replaced with motorbikes, but the white *matatus* still dominate the roads. Pedestrians weave their way through major intersections crawling with vehicles. Somehow, the traffic flows through unmarked lanes and operates in the absence of traffic lights.

When we walked through town this morning to shop for school supplies we would use for the book project, my city sense kicked in and I remembered how to maneuver the chaos – you just keep moving with confidence like you know where you are going. Walking through New York, Atlanta, DC, London and Paris with Adam and Benjamin at younger ages was good preparation for hustling through the streets of Kampala. I was surprised at how calm I felt holding the hands of my 10- and 12-year-old boys, as we dodged cars and street vendors.

Later I realized that my disposition was not only an outcrop of faith, but also a sign of my age and life experience. The fears and uncertainties I harbored when living here before were natural for a young female residing in a foreign country. And perhaps this time I was encouraged by the marked increase of available goods and products. There were visible signs of development and the city pace seemed to project overall improvement of life conditions. As we walked the streets I was looking for "what's new"; I was not looking for "what could go wrong."

The streets were lined with shops displaying everything from housewares, fabrics, and hardware, to sophisticated grocery stores. Kampala had certainly changed over the years. Everyone carried cell phones, and young women, especially, dressed in more western styles – including tight jeans.

My Bitter Lemon soda brought back a flood of memories. It had been my favorite soft drink and it is not available in the US. As memories surfaced, so did all the epiphanies I have written about. I wondered whether this revisit would affirm lessons I had learned from seeds planted long ago and whether our children would experience many of the same ah-has. I thought about our old friends. Would they be as excited to see us as we would be to see them? What would be different in Ibanda? How is Job? The last communication from Job (eight months ago) worried me, as he did not sound well. He expressed in an email, "I am now a man of the streets." What in the heck did that mean? There are no streets and there is no homelessness in the village. I also thought about Habitat and what impact it might have had in the village – knowing that it had stopped operating there a few years ago, but not understanding the full story as to why the project had gone awry.

I looked up from the window and there was Mugisha.

"Carrie . . . Carrie . . . ," Mugisha sang as he stretched out his arms to pull me in. Except that he is a bit heavier and has a few additional wisdom lines around the eyes and temples, Mugisha looks the same as we left him 15 years ago.

Mugisha greeted me European style: three hugs, alternating right and left cheeks. His mountain guide experience had given him plenty of friends from Britain, Germany and France. During the time we were neighbors, Mugisha spent quite a bit of time in the mountains, leading tourists on an eight-day trek to and from Margherita Peak.

"Betty couldn't come today. She has to work. She and the children look forward to receiving you tomorrow at our home in Kampala." As excited as I felt to see Mugisha, who had emailed regularly with me about our entire trip logistics, I couldn't wait to see Betty.

"Do you remember Johnson?" Mugisha asked as he introduced the man he had brought with him. "Yes, I do," I responded as I reached out to shake his hand, saying, "*Wabukiri.*" Johnson's smile turned to a familiar chuckle, a common response to foreigners speaking Lukonzo. Mugisha explained that Johnson is a "cousin-brother" and that he would be our driver for the month. We had not known Johnson well, but we knew of him. I was pleased that we would have a *mukonzo* from Ibanda as our driver and guide.

The three of us sat down at the bar and had a soda together. Mugisha and I shared constant smiles as we reminisced about living in Ibanda, remembering the same but also different stories of Rwanzo and Benard (he and Betty's toddler.) "Benard is now 17 and is in S4 at a secondary boarding school in Kampala!" Mugisha said as he raised his eyebrows in disbelief.

"Where have the years gone?" I replied, as I showed him photos in the album I had brought to share with friends.

I was still amazed that after ten years of silence between us, (we lost touch when we moved to South Africa) Mugisha emailed us out of the blue, "Bob and Carrie, are you there? Is this your email address?" His first email came a month after we had made the decision to travel to Uganda. For me, the communication with Mugisha was the first in a long series of affirmations that we were supposed to be making this trip. Mugisha and I had become reacquainted through a year and a half of emails: sharing personal, family and career turns that have shaped our lives over the past 15 years. We had even become prayerfully involved months earlier when his nine-year-old daughter Benadette was diagnosed with a brain tumor. We were also pleased to help with surgery expenses by advancing money as a deposit for their home in Ibanda, which we would rent during our village stay. Bob and I anticipated a heartfelt reunion with Betty, Mugisha and Benard, and looked forward to meeting Benadette and their one-year-old, Benita.

Before leaving Kampala, we visited Mugisha and Betty and their kids at Betty's workplace. Having taught primary school for several years, Betty switched to hairdressing a few years ago and now works at a salon in Kampala.

She and her kids stay in a small room in the back of the salon, while Mugisha stays mostly in their house in the village – eight hours away. Many people working in Kampala have left families back in their home villages in order to have jobs.

Our visit was lovely and was the first of many reunions with old friends. The fact that they would all come to Ibanda to host us made our brief encounter sufficient. Betty had prepared food for us. We were served a plate of avocados, pineapples, and mangoes, followed by a bowl of peas and rice. It was Adam and Benjamin's first time experiencing Ugandan hospitality, a cultural trait that would favorably color their whole experience.

When the day came for us to travel to Ibanda, we were well rested and ready to dive into village life. Over several days we had spent 20 hours on the road, and though Uganda's countryside is scenic, we were tired of moving around and being spectators. By this time, we had gotten to know Johnson pretty well and had enjoyed learning in-depth customs of the Bakonzo tribe from him. Some of his stories about birthing, marriage and burial were familiar to me, but many were new.

I was particularly intrigued by child naming customs. I had understood long ago that birth order determines a baby's first name, but I was not aware that people later receive proverbial and situational names. For instance, if it has been a heavy rainy season or if a child is born when the father is on safari, he would receive a name that carries those meanings.

Johnson is called *Bwambale* Johnson *Muthahinga*. Muthahinga was a nickname for Johnson's grandfather which got passed down to all of his grandchildren. It means "man doesn't dig." Johnson's grandfather had two wives, and the second complained about her husband's lack of participation in helping with the garden. His supposed favoritism towards his first wife and lack of support for his second warranted him this name. Situational names are one way of keeping generational stories alive.

The first born male is called *Baluku* and the second born male is *Bwambale*. Therefore, we were bringing Baluku Adam and Bwambale Benjamin to Ibanda. We had no idea upon entering the village how well received these two basungu children with Lukonzo names would be.

After two hours on the tarmac road from Fort Portal, we reached the turnoff for Ibanda. Many old and several new signs were posted at the corner, indicating the development projects that are located within the twelve-kilometer stretch of road up to the base of Rwenzori National Park. Habitat for Humanity, ADRA, US AID, Catholic Church, WWF, UNDP – everything from women's cooperatives to a Norwegian-sponsored water project – it appeared that there were many development efforts taking place in the villages. The big mango tree on the opposite side of the road shaded numerous people awaiting public transportation to take them to Fort Portal or Kasese, the two nearest towns.

As we turned on to the dirt road, our vehicle became a time capsule, taking us back not only the 18 years since our initial entry into the village, but generations back into Konzo culture. Our return to the village would also plant seeds for future generations: seeds in our children, as well as the people God would connect us to during our stay. In addition, seeing the village through the eyes of our children would close the time gap between past and future, in the sheer beauty of "present-ness" that children are able to capture.

Sensing the anxiety filling our van, Johnson said, "Here we go Wagners! Welcome Back!"

I scooted a couple of inches forward in my seat and sat upright with my camera on my lap. My eyes widened with wonder. From my position in the front seat, I looked at Adam and Benjamin, seated on the middle bench with their heads out the windows on opposite sides of the van. Adam was taking pictures as we drove. Bob was in the back next to Benadette and Benard, whom we had collected on our way back through Kampala. They had made the last ten hours of the journey with us.

I wished that Bob was sitting next to me so that I could squeeze his hand to share the intense emotions of the drive. When I looked back at him, he gave me that squeeze through his eyes. His eyes also said, "I love you, sweetness." I returned his endearment with a smile.

The road seemed longer than I remembered; it felt as if we were moving in slow motion. I thanked God once again for giving us this opportunity to return blessings on a community who had so blessed our lives. I asked for His guidance on every aspect of our stay. I prayed for Job and all the old friends we would see in the village, and I prayed that we would accomplish what God had brought us here to do, even though we didn't know exactly what that might be.

"Ladies and Gentlemen, I would like to turn our meeting over to Mr. Bob Wagner who is visiting with his family." Stephen introduced us, placing his hand on Bob's shoulder and nodding his head towards the rest of us. "We are very fortunate that they will be with us for two weeks, joining in our soccer programs and visiting lots of other people, schools and development efforts. Let's welcome them with applause."

The room was small but accommodated the 20 of us, all seated in white plastic chairs. We sat in the sitting room of a brick house in Ibanda trading center – the place where Stephen meets with his soccer staff every Friday night.

Fifteen dark faces studied Bob as he began his little speech. Bob expressed our gratitude for having been sponsored to make this trip, and he acknowledged the many donors back home who had contributed the equipment which now filled a bedroom in Stephen's village house. As Bob was explaining why we have hearts for Ibanda, he talked about the Ugandan friendships we had made and have maintained over the years.

"In 1992, we moved to Ibanda into a house near here," Bob said as he waved his hand to the right. He paused and then waved his hand to the left and said slowly as he pondered his placement, "I guess . . . it was more. . . that way."

All eyes and ears were fixed on Bob as his head began to rotate up, down and around, looking at the walls of our meeting room. I didn't know what he was doing until he blurted out in a high pitched voice, "It was here! This is our house!"

I could not believe that we were sitting in our old house, but as soon as he spoke, I recognized the room. Everyone laughed while we gazed at the details of the windows, which were now glass rather than the wooden shutters that we had used. The white walls had also disguised the room; they were not the creamy yellow we had painted. We had entered the room from the back door, in darkness, so we had no clue that we were entering a significant place, and the backyard of this house had changed so much that we didn't recognize it either. Bob had explained to Stephen on the phone where we had lived, but the exact place also didn't register with him.

"Welcome to our house!" Bob continued.

"Were any of you in the nursery school next door when you were young?" I asked as I looked at the young adults who surrounded us. Several people raised their hands.

"Do you remember the basungu living in this house?" I asked.

"I do," Juliette said, "And I remember you had a big dog."

"Perhaps you were among the children who used to throw rocks at Rwanzo!" I responded. We all laughed again.

This happened our third night in the village and began many déjà vu experiences which would keep us laughing and occasionally crying throughout our time in Ibanda.

When we got home that night, we lit our lanterns and took a cold splash bath from a bucket of river water, just as Bob and I used to do. We brushed our teeth under the moonlit sky, spitting our toothpaste on the ground, which was covered with banana tree fiber. After making one last visit to our outdoor pit latrine, we settled the kids into their beds under their mosquito nets, said prayers with them, and crawled under our own mosquito net. I drifted to sleep, smiling at the sense of peace blanketing me.

Each day pulled us a little deeper into the flow of village life. Along the way, we were blessed by personal interactions and challenged by the obstacles intrinsic to poverty environments. As if rafting down an old but familiar river, Bob and I felt at home in the setting, yet fully aware of the unpredictable nature of life in a subsistent culture. I love the way Bob captured the nostalgia in his journal:

"The rooster crows, wind rustles the banana leaves, someone is chopping firewood nearby, a motorcycle speeds up the dirt road, a radio crackles with an African language, the "klug-klug" of water emptying from a jerry can. Suddenly the sun pops over the mountains facing our window. Morning in the village. It comes alive slowly and gradually picks up speed until later in the day when life is bustling all about. I love this time of day.

Back in Ibanda after 15 years. It feels like a dream, a time warp. Some friends have died, some are grey or have lost hair, some have put on weight, but many don't look much different. How odd and how wonderful. It almost feels like we never left or that only a little time has passed. But we know in those 15 years there are stories of calamity, good fortune, heartache and happiness, sickness and health. Carrie and I have our share of stories too. It's been wonderful, intense, fascinating and mostly joyful catching up with our friends of long ago."

Adam and Benjamin's entry to the village was also pleasant. Initially timid, though trusting mom and dad to guide them, within two days our children went from toe dipping to full immersion. They tried new foods, rode on the backs of motorcycles up the village road, played with lots of kids and greeted everyone in Lukonzo. Their reaction to being the center of attention transitioned from feeling annoyed and frustrated to feeling special and honored. This same transition had taken over a year for me and Bob to make in 1991. Of course, adults have much more "baggage" to weed through, but there is beauty in children's naiveté: they don't analyze things to death.

I was intrigued by Benjamin's observations and perceptions of poverty. He put it this way:

"By living like the people, we are learning more about poverty. Poverty means more work – and they don't complain about it. They carry 5-10 gallons of water from the river in jerry cans. They also grow their own food, slaughter chickens, cut down trees and chop fire wood, hand wash clothes, iron clothes with hot coals and chop down bananas. We take for granted the luxury of having electricity, having things done for us – and purified water. Most things we have, we take for granted. We live a comfy life back home."

"Mom, is this how it was when you lived here?" Benjamin asked as we walked up the road to our house. I thought for a moment.

"The way of life is remarkably the same – the way people dress, cook, eat and relate to one another. The mountains are even more beautiful than I remember. The visible changes include widespread use of cell phones, motorcycles used for taxis, and more brick houses than mud and wattle shacks. Those are the biggest changes I can see. These are significant improvements when you consider that we had no phones back then. Improved communication and transportation can dramatically influence a community's livelihood."

I thought for a second more and then exclaimed, "Oh, and the bridge! There are lots more vehicles moving up and down and across the river. That's just incredible and so wonderful to see. Benjamin, what do you like about this place?"

Benjamin looked up to the mountains and then confidently greeted pedestrians coming towards us, "*Wabukiri, yirewahe?*" (Hello. How's it?) Smiling from ear to ear, the two women carrying bunches of bananas on their backs returned the greeting and cheerfully chatted about the little white boy speaking their language.

After the women moved on, Benjamin thought before he answered my question, and then responded sincerely, "I like the beautiful views of the mountains. I like playing soccer with the kids and making friends. But mostly, I like the people: their characters, their kindness and hospitality. At first I was embarrassed to be stared at and called mzungu so much, but then I realized that they were just curious and didn't know what to say to me. I think me and Adam are the only white kids they have ever seen. I like it here."

When we reached our home, kids were playing soccer in our back compound with a ball made from banana fibers (the most common ball around the village). Benjamin quickly joined in the play. Adam picked coffee beans from a coffee tree in our yard and Bob and Mugisha talked on the back stoop of our house. I went into the house and found Benita roaming from room to room. I scooped her up, wiped her runny nose and gave her a little cuddle before I put her out in the backyard with the other kids.

I had a few household chores to do: boil the next day's supply of drinking water and organize the stationery supplies we would take for tomorrow's school visit. As I listened to the children laughing outside my kitchen window, I thought about how nice it is that children play outside with each other, an aspect of life that is sometimes lost in over-electrified societies. Moments later, I was completely frustrated that my camera battery was again drained.

I would have to take the battery and charger back down to the trading center and leave it at one of the shops that has electricity.

Playing soccer every afternoon with school kids was certainly a highlight for Adam and Benjamin. Playing sports together offered opportunities for friendship that crossed cultural and language barriers. Stephen was a great host for our children, giving them technical instruction and expecting them to fully participate in his programs, which span schools throughout the large mountainous area. They participated at numerous schools.

The final and pinnacle soccer event during our village stay was an all-day soccer tournament that engaged 150 players from surrounding villages. Each team played seven games that day. The field was filled with the colorful uniforms we had brought from Asheville. Many kids were putting on football boots (soccer cleats) for the first time. The day was filled with action, excitement and new experiences for everyone.

Bob and I were glad for our kids to have fun playing soccer, but we also valued the relationships they were building. During their walks to and from soccer fields, Stephen got to know our boys, and he talked openly about his experiences living in the village. He was respectful of their youth by choosing appropriate topics to discuss; however, he also honored their maturity by not sugar-coating the ugly truths of corruption.

One example of Stephen's authenticity took place as we were driving to visit a school. As we were driving down the road, a large group of kids walked up the road towards us. Adam asked Stephen, "Where are those kids going?"

Stephen responded with a disgusted tone, "That ticks me off! Those kids are going back to their homes up the mountain."

"Where are they coming from," I asked.

"From the church. The church was given money to build and operate an orphanage, but church leaders are using the building for other purposes. International visitors have been here this week to do a program evaluation, so the parish staff rounded up children to fill the building. The visitors probably were fooled that their mission and purposes were being fulfilled. So now they have left and the children are sent away. It just stinks!"

This event sparked a great conversation with our kids about the complexities of poverty, development and international intervention. Bob and I shared stories about times that we had lost respect for people involved in corrupted operations. Additionally, we expressed that over time we had learned how difficult it is to discern the truth in many situations. Generally, doubt proceeds trust.

They say a picture is worth a thousand words. I say a million.

The images that have been etched in my heart over the years are the same ones that took us back into the heart of the village. The photographs we took to share with people, known and unknown to us, bridged the time and cultural gap, connecting us personally to a wide range of people throughout the mountains surrounding Ibanda. My photo album was like a passport with a resident status stamp; it took us into people's homes and opened the door for personal conversations and authentic portrait photography. The photographs surfaced memories and evoked emotions.

We first shared the pictures with Betty, Mugisha and Johnson. They helped us identify people in the photos whom we had not known. Our photographs included young and old from far and wide in the Mobuku valley as well as the surrounding mountains. On several occasions Job had taken us deep into the mountains to photograph Habitat homeowners and to attend events rich with cultural traditions, like Bakonzo music, dancing, and cooking.

Johnson was especially helpful in finding people in the photos as he drove the vehicle, scanning faces for familiarity. Several times, he abruptly stopped the vehicle and spoke to pedestrians that he thought had some relation to people in the photographs. Then, he would pull over, park the vehicle, and together we would follow someone through the tall grass to a home site. The mysterious appearance of a white person approaching one's compound was quickly explained when I greeted in Lukonzo and handed over the picture. Faces lit up: some of them responding to the first photograph they had ever seen of themselves.

Other times, I instigated the abrupt stop, exclaiming, "Stop Johnson. I see somebody I know!" This happened the first time we drove into Ibanda trading center. I recognized the "Boy with Branch", one of the little boys in my *Portraits of Uganda* photo exhibit. Erisa Musabali, now 20 years old, drives a motorcycle taxi and aspires to drive a vehicle one day. He has the same face and the same mischievous, yet playful smile. I remember him running around the village, using sticks for guns and peeking around the banana trees at us.

Equally fulfilling as giving people pictures of themselves from long ago, was the joy in showing them their picture on the LCD screen of my digital camera.

Johnson's mother laughed when she looked at herself in my replay screen on the back of my camera. I asked Johnson what she was laughing about.

She said in Lukonzo, "Oh,…is that how I look?" Johnson and I laughed too and I thought, wouldn't it be nice to be among a society that places such little value on self image. In the Western world, we are terribly consumed by what we look like. It's a pity to me that so much of our time and resources are spent on how we look. I thought further to how vanity obsession has impacted health and relationships in our societies, even to the point of eating disorders and excessive cosmetic surgery. I expressed my disappointment about this cultural development to Johnson, which in turn stimulated another loaded discussion about cultural differences.

"Johnson, what do you see as the major cultural differences between the Bakonzo and bazungu?"

"Well, in fact, you people are honest. We Africans have a habit of not telling the full truth. We do not want to disappoint someone with negative news and we do not want to deface another by revealing something they have done wrong. White people are truthful and up front in their assessments."

I thought Johnson's perspective was interesting – and honest.

"Johnson, you have guided American, German, French and British tourists for years. What do you find funny about Americans and Europeans?"

"We think it's funny that you live so privately. You close the doors to your homes. When we mountain guides take tourists up, we invite them to sit with us around our fire and take *obundu* (staple food made from cassava flour) with us. Some join us for a cup of tea, but then they are quick to huddle back to themselves. I have grown used to bazungu's need for privacy, but many Bakonzo would not understand this thing. We also think it's funny that a man helps out in the kitchen and with other household chores. But these days we are also starting to develop. Our modern generation of men is learning to cook. And women are finding more places in schools and the workforce."

"Is the cultural shift in roles good?" I asked.

Johnson's response revealed the dichotomy felt by many of us as it pertains to developing societies, "Well, we are sad to see the loss of traditions that have made us who we are. But we are happy to see improvements in our way of living."

This and other discussions on culture with our Ugandan friends were a highlight of my village stay.

During our term with Habitat, our discussions focused on house construction, family selection, and house payments. We missed opportunities for more personal disclosure.

This trip was all about relationships – a fact that shaped our time into leisurely visits, shared meals and intimate sharing. We were able to have discussions we had always wanted to have with these friends. We discussed politics, faith, and parenting.

We even talked about sex and birth control. I was most amused at our friend Nelson's reaction to seeing our children. He laughed and told me, "Adam looks like Bob and Benjamin looks like you, Carrie. In our culture, we say that the parent whom the child takes after is the one who was the strongest during conception." A little embarrassed by his comment, I laughed and felt privileged to gain an inside cultural perspective. Nelson's sense of humor is what I remembered most about him. It seemed like just yesterday that we had hiked two hours to his church in Isule, listening to him tell funny stories along the way.

On this trip, we picked up right where we had left off with Nelson. Nelson's other name, *KiKunki* means bellybutton, and has a full story supporting the meaning. Nelson gave me six handwritten pages of Bakonzo namesakes and generational history. He seemed delighted to host us at his church again and expressed on behalf of his congregation how honored they felt to have been chosen out of hundreds of churches in the area as our place for worship.

Carrie, Kesi Bweya, Bwanandeke, and Nelson KiKundi

Yodesi Biira, 1991

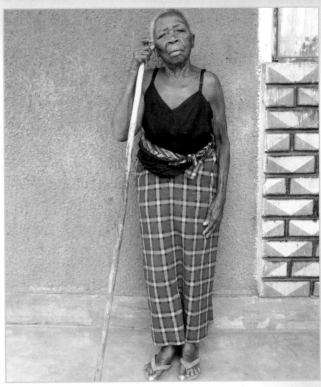

Yodesi Biira, 2009

Yodesi and Carrie, 2009

Mugisha, Betty, Mbusa and Benard, 1993

Betty and Carrie, 2009

Benjamin, Benita, Adam, Bennadette, and Mugisha, 2009

Our neighbor Tom, the tailor, 1992

Tom, 2009

Bob with our yard boy, Tom and his brother, Nyasyo, the carpenter, 1994

Pastor Tom, 2009

Kumaraki John, Ellen and their daughters, 1994

Ellen and Kumaraki and their youngest, 2009

Jane, Jahard, and Job, 1993

Job and Jahard, 2009

Benard and Carrie, 1992

Adam, Benard and Benjamin, 2009

Kumaraki's mom in her kitchen, 1992

Kumaraki's parents, 2009

Nyasyo, Bwanandeke, Carrie and Wilfred, in front of Bwanandeke's house, 1993

Bob and Carrie with Kilembe Secondary School teachers, Stephen, Stephen, Bwanandeke, Stanley, and Edward, 2009

Our neighbor Mbabazi and her children, 1993   Mbabazi, 2009

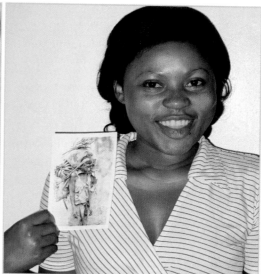

Florence Nyamungu, 1993   Florence's granddaughter, Tujabe Maureen, 2009

Erisa Musabali, 1993   Erisa Musabali, 2009

On our second day in Ibanda, we had plans to visit Bwanandeke and his family. Through an email, Bwanandeke had invited us to come to his home on July 9 at 11 am. In the same email, he suggested that we go and visit Job directly after lunch on the same day.

My anticipation of reuniting with two treasured friends made the morning seem long, although without electricity, our morning routine would take every bit of three hours.

Before we had finished preparing to leave our house, I was surprised by a man who entered through our back door and was standing in our dining room. I looked at him for a brief moment, as I didn't recognize him instantly.

"Carrie! I'm happy to see you!"

As soon as he opened his mouth revealing a distinguished gap between his two front teeth, I knew it was Bwanandeke. Once I recognized him, I realized that he did look the same – but I had not expected him to come to our home; we were going to his. Bwanendeke and I hugged and laughed and studied each other. Then we hugged again.

I later learned from Johnson how unnatural hugging is for the Bakonzo. I asked Johnson how people greet each other when they haven't seen each other in a long time. Johnson replied in an African way, trying to make me feel comfortable, by saying, "We hug." I confronted his statement by dropping my chin and raising my eyebrows. Finally, he was truthful in saying, "In fact… Bakonzo don't hug. We don't hug." We laughed – at his statement and at his honesty.

Perhaps Bwanandeke was trying to greet appropriately in my cultural body language: regardless of intent, the excitement to see each other was mutual.

"We were just about to come to your house," I said, looking at my watch to see if we were running late. Bwanandeke assured me that we were within time but that he wanted to check that we are okay, (in other words, he couldn't wait to see us). I was reminded of Bwanandeke's unusual punctuality and how much I had appreciated his acts of kindness for us when we lived here before.

While the kids finished getting ready, Bob and I sat with Bwanandeke and reminisced. An intelligent man with a college degree, Bwanandeke can be quite serious and analytical. He had been the project manager for Habitat in Ibanda for several years and now teaches at Kilembe Secondary School.

He also has a great laugh and attentiveness to details. Bob and I have fond memories of hours upon hours discussing poverty and development issues with Bwanandeke and the Habitat committee.

We had talked only a few minutes when I looked out our front window and saw another man approaching. He had on a wide brimmed hat, similar to a cowboy hat, but more typical of what people in Africa wear on safari in game parks. He walked quickly with an expression of certainty as he passed the front window and rounded the corner to come around back.

"That's Job! Bob, Job's here!" I exclaimed as I jumped up and hurried to the back door. I stepped outside just in time to see Job round the back corner of our house. He was wearing a big smile, and laughed the moment he saw me.

I'm not sure which one of us initiated the hug because it happened so fast and so naturally. And we too studied each other, looking for changes and signs of age. I could see that his hair had grayed by his sideburns, which protruded from his hat. Other than that, Job looked the same. We smiled as our eyes travelled each other's features.

"You have a new hat, Job."

"Yes."

Then we began our Lukonzo greetings that he had taught us long ago. "*Wabukire. Abanabanayo?*" (Good morning. How is your family?)

"*Ehhh, Banayondeke,*" (The family is fine), Job replied and continued, "Ah, you still speak the language?"

I smiled and said, "We had a good teacher."

Job came in for a cup of tea and joined Bwanandeke on the couch to look through the photo album. Job squinted his eyes as he looked at the pictures and said, "I can't see well these days. I can hardly read my Bible anymore. Taking the reading glasses off of my head and handing them to Job, I said, "Here, try these." Job put my glasses on and said, "Ah ha… this is better." My prescription is not an exact fit for Job's vision, but my glasses did help. Seeing the two of them sitting in our house, laughing and sharing memories, was a moment that Bob and I will cherish forever.

I had not intended to tell them about this book just yet; however, when I began explaining the purposes of our trip, Bwanandeke interrupted me, "I have seen."

He opened our trip folder and pulled out the flyer we had used for trip fundraising. In the brief time that I had gone to meet Job at the back door, Bwanandeke had looked through everything on our coffee table, including all of our travel logistics and the book outline.

Oh well, the cat's out of the bag, I thought, shifting my attention quickly to Job's reaction as Bwanandeke retrieved the paper and read, "*The Book of Job*, by Carrie Wagner." Bwanandeke chuckled as he read the title, but Job sat silent, his countenance displaying an inquisitive smile. (*The Book of Job* was the original title of this book.)

"Well Job, what do you think? How does this make you feel?"

Job hesitated as he thought and then responded, "It's good. Yeah. It's good." Job appeared honored that I would title a book after him, but his humility masked any excitement or anticipation about what the book contained.

We talked a little more about the book and how we would spend our two weeks in the village, then gathered ourselves to walk to Bwanandeke's home.

We were anxious to see the bridge and to see Job's and Bwanandeke's families.

"Put your foot here," Job said to Adam. Job had already carried our bags and cameras across the river and had assisted Bob, me, and Benjamin through the rushing water. Up to Adam's thighs in some spots, the water seemed high for dry season. Adam pulled his shorts up and held on to Job's hand as his feet tested for stable rocks in the river bed. Children dressed in purple school uniforms waited on the other side of the river, reaching their hands out to assist us as well.

We crossed the river in this fashion to give Adam and Benjamin an appreciation for what life was like before the bridge was built. Job explained to them the tremendous impact the bridge has made on the communities of Ibanda and Kyanya. In fact, earlier in the week, many of our Habitat colleagues had expressed not only gratitude for the bridge, but also for Habitat houses and the cooperative ideas that we had shared with them. Stanley Baluku talked about a youth project that he had modeled after our group savings methodology. The Grameen Bank style of micro-credit financing was also useful to Bwanandeke and his coffee growers' cooperative. Bwanandeke explained, "Before Habitat, we thought that the only way to get a loan was as an individual through the bank. That was impossible for most of us. Working together and creating a group savings fund has made our coffee cooperative successful. As a group, we process and ship 50 tons of coffee per season."

During our visits with Job, Bwanandeke and other friends, we expressed appreciation for each other. Bob and I took the opportunity to thank them for the years they had hosted us. In turn, they expressed how they had appreciated us living among them – village style. We were touched by their words. We interpreted their sentiments as appreciating us for who we are, not just that we brought Habitat to their communities. The warmth with which we were received has stamped our hearts and (our children's) for a lifetime.

On our last day in the village, our family climbed to the top of a huge boulder. Adam and Benjamin had climbed to the top earlier in the week and wanted to show their parents the incredible views of the mountains and valley from that vantage point. Bob commented that we had never climbed this boulder before, but remembered there always being kids up there, looking down on us.

Our children were right. The view was spectacular. As I looked up to the dark blue Rwenzoris, backlit by a melting sun, I released a range of emotions which had been caged by my subconscious. Over the course of two weeks, I had been so involved in visiting old friends, taking pictures, watching Adam and Benjamin play soccer, administering the school visits, and processing my children's reactions to poverty and immersive living in the village, that I had suppressed my own emotions.

For a brief moment, I was able to tune out all of the surrounding distractions: children laughing, pedestrians looking at the white adults on top of the big rock, and motorbikes vrooming up the dusty road. Bob and I used to sit on a rock in the middle of the Mobuku River seeking this type of solitude. Somehow, I had found it in the midst of everything happening around me.

The gentle breeze crackling through the banana tree branches reminded me that my maker is ever-present, and was indeed responsible for the amazing time that we had spent in Ibanda. I thanked Him by smiling at my children, who were giggling and playing with new Ugandan friends.

Bob and I had been amazed at how well Adam and Benjamin adjusted to life without their usual amenities. And even though they each had challenging experiences – both had bouts of diarrhea, Benjamin had two battles with bed bugs, and they both witnessed a case of deceptive corruption within a church-run orphanage – they maintained a favorable impression of their time in the village. I was pleased that Adam and Benjamin had a taste of conflict but still valued the richness of culture more than the problems of poverty. I felt proud of my sons.

I was incredibly relieved that Job is okay. Still struggling with effects of poverty and personal health issues, he continues to find his strength in God. His exemplary character traits are just as I remembered. His service to the community continues as he is chairman of another bridge committee seeking funding for a footbridge much higher in the mountains. His laugh and gentle spirit made the days we spent with him a delight. Watching Job teach my children how to eat obundu and how to cross the river are impressions that will be etched in my heart forever.

I also felt overwhelmed with gratitude. More than we could have imagined, God guided our steps, protected us, deepened old friendships and built new ones. The warm welcome and authenticity of relationships affirmed our need to return to Uganda. The worry I had harbored about losing touch with people had been replaced with peace. We had kept in touch with many friends through written letters for several years following our departure in 1994, but eventually that communication dried up. Now I felt assured that these are indeed lifetime friends. Our Ugandan friends embraced us as if our revisit had restored hope in them – hope that caring relationships, of young and old, can be shared with friends across the ocean.

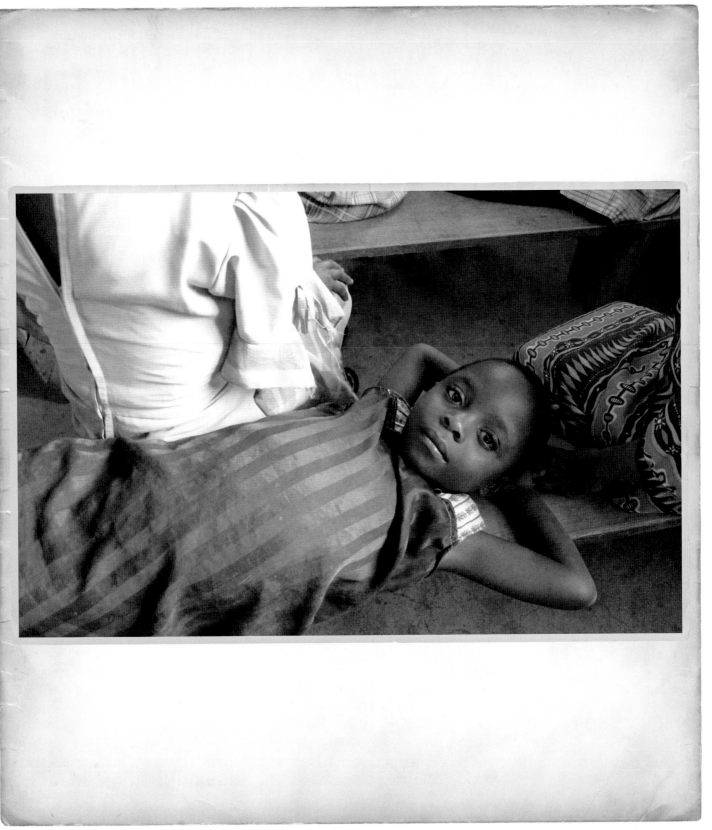

"Passengers, please take your seats, buckle your seatbelts and prepare for departure."

Our preparation for takeoff had been smooth, but relatively mechanical. I was focused on the logistics of travel, not my emotions. We travelled for two days and spent our last night with friends in Kampala, squeezing in one last visit.

We left for the airport at 5:00 am, our luggage packed for safe travel; this time instead of soccer equipment, our bags contained crafts for which we would seek an American market. We had taken our daily malaria pill, checked our luggage at the British Airways counter and gone through customs with no hassles.

My only regret was not having the opportunity to say a proper goodbye to Johnson. He dropped us at "Departures" and went to park the vehicle. He was intending to come back in to say goodbye, but when he got there, he found that non-passengers were not allowed in the terminal. Thankfully Johnson saw us standing near the window and came to bid us farewell through the glass. I wanted to hug him and thank him for all he had done. He had spent 30 days driving us around Uganda, and had taken extra care to assure the vehicle was safe. We had shared many discussions. He had participated in the school visits with us. He had become Uncle Johnson to Adam and Benjamin.

I looked at Johnson, trying to show appreciation through my eyes. He understood my expression and placed both of his hands against the window. I put my hands up against his and "hugged" him through the glass. That was our goodbye.

Bob did hug Johnson, as he went back through security to receive a letter Johnson had written to us. I packed the letter in my carry-on and waited until we boarded the plane to open it.

As we took off, I glanced at the African landscape stretching far beyond the wing of the plane. I imagined all of the people we had seen and the experiences we had enjoyed. I knew that I had left a piece of myself behind and that I was taking pieces of so many others with me. The emptiness I had felt the last time I departed Uganda had been transformed into fullness.

I read Johnson's letter before I fell asleep. His words encapsulated the authentic friendships we left behind. But this time our departure felt more like a beginning than an end. I had peace that we had planted seeds for long-term relationships and had harvested fruits of seeds planted long ago. Adam expressed in his journal, *"Uganda is a beautiful place that still needs development, but it has me captured. I'm already planning to come back."*

Dear Carrie and Bob,

I am so thankful to you (Wagners) for having come back to Uganda and Ibanda in particular. Sixteen years is a long period for you to have remembered us. It is because you love us and it has been our joy to see you and your children.

I greatly thank all those women, men, and children in the USA who contributed a lot of items, money and moral support. I greatly commend their generosity and I tend to believe that it was God working through them. May Almighty God bless them abundantly (Acts 20:35).

In the Konzo culture, when a young couple progresses in their family and when they get a second child, they (the parents) take their children to their grandparents. We call it *eriyahya* (to go and eat with parents) as an indication that they are thankful to have enabled them to marry and that they are fertile/ fruitful. Therefore, your coming to us for the purpose of showing us your children is a fulfillment of the above cultural norm of the Bakonzo of which you didn't know. When one goes to eriyahya, the couple go with a huge fatty goat and gifts for the parents. And this is what you did. You brought us sports equipment, photos of many people, gifts to intimate friends, visiting women organizations, the scholarships you gave, and a collection of crafts to show the people in the USA.

You have wonderful boys Baluku Adam and Bwambale Benjamin. They are great children, very innovative, friendly, and easy to make friends, full of amusement, with outgoing and open minded attitudes, and above all – God fearing. What wonderful children! May God bless them and you the parents as you do everything possible in bringing them up.

Your visit and the association through interactions has impacted me in such a way that the way you think and evaluate situations, the love you have for the people and your own children has given me a challenge and homework for me to do. Yes, whites have shown love and given out tokens of assistance to individuals, organizations, yes, but they have not shown the kind of love and commitment and the zeal to assist people as you have.

May God Bless You,
Johnson Bwambale Mutahinga

As I send this book to press, having reviewed the stories and images one last time, I begin the process of letting go. This piece of work has truly been a labor of love. Similar to Adam's comments when leaving Uganda, the feelings pushing my pen are "bittersweet."

The bitterness lies in the fact that this part of my journey is over and once again I face a crossroad, looking for what's next. In order to move on, I will have to emerge from this place where I have been immersed mentally, physically and spiritually for the past three years. I have learned that I cannot immerse in two places at the same time. Where God wants me next is unknown to me now, but I'm sure it will be revealed.

The sweetness surpasses the bitterness tenfold. While the trip was a milestone for our family development, stretching and strengthening each of us and our relationships with each other, the nine months of trip preparation was equally transformational.

A year ago, Bob and I apprehensively mailed our first fundraising letter for the mission trip. We had budgeted and set goals that felt impossible, especially during a global economic recession. By May we had met our fundraising goal – nearly to the penny. Each fundraising event embodied nuggets of wisdom and divine connections.

Our church-wide rummage sale was a lesson in "Trash and Treasure". We spent six months cleaning out every closet and drawer in our home, filling our garage with things that could be used by others. Taking boxes of games, toys, clothes and unused household items to the church sale was a cleansing exercise, enhanced by the joy of giving. After the sale, which raised $1500, the church donated two truckloads of stuff to our local Habitat for Humanity and Good Will Industries. This event had particular impact on Adam, who like his mother, tends to collect too much stuff.

The benefit concert dinner, which raised $1,000 for CDTS, was an exercise in "Simple, Decent and Affordable." The dinner was an eclectic but beautiful blend of African cuisine, piano and bluegrass music, and a presentation on Uganda. The beauty of the evening came from the many volunteers who gave of themselves by cooking, serving, decorating, performing and hosting.

I have learned that this book is merely a byproduct of something much bigger: God has used the book as a platform to further mold me and my family. Though many seasons may pass before our children bear fruit from the seeds planted in them, we can already see how the village experience has impacted their global perspectives. The seeds of village wisdom, planted in me long ago, have been clarified and nurtured through my writing. I share these lessons with the hope of shaping our children's values and of inspiring others to seek their own transformational experiences.

Afterword

Everyone has a story. It's in the intersections of our stories (our relationships) where the spice of life is found. And those intersections can be a near miss, unless we travel with our heads up, looking for connections. I call it "connecting the dots." When people ask me how this project came together, I share a different piece of the story, (a dot), which in isolation is "just a good story," but in connection with numerous other dots, is absolutely divine. The pieces to my story (the connected dots) each involve a little piece of another person's story. Sharing our stories with each other not only inspires and encourages us on our life paths, but also reveals the connections between us.

I am reminded of the eight years following our time living in Uganda. We spent five years at the international headquarters of Habitat for Humanity International, frequently traveling worldwide, and an additional three years in South Africa. The rewards and fulfillment from those years are nestled in the stories shared by people across the globe. Our HFHI co-workers were from many countries. All of them had amazing stories from working cross-culturally and stretching their personal comfort zones. Stories were often entertaining; for example, the stories about varmint intrusions or language goof-ups. Other stories shared were more personal: events or happenings that brought us to tears, or put us to shame, or brought us into the utter presence of God. These shared stories became the common bond for everlasting friendships.

The original vision for *Village Wisdom* was a photography book. But as I scanned the images and began preparing the *Portraits of Uganda* photography collection, events and emotions resurfaced so vividly that I had to write. Seeing the faces of people who had impacted our lives in such a powerful way gave me renewed vision for the book and inspired my purpose for writing. I realized then that the purposes for writing my story are threefold.

The first purpose is to honor and give gratitude to Job and many others like him – from far and near corners of the world – people who live under difficult conditions and suffer, in part, as a result of the imbalance of world resources.

To our dear Ugandan friends,

I thank you from the bottom of my heart for sharing your lives with me and my family. You have read in these pages the impact that living with you has had on our lives. Now I have shared with you (and many others) how meaningful our cross-cultural friendships were and continue to be. And hopefully through my honest account, you have come to appreciate that mzungu simply means white skin. Bazungu, though influenced by Western culture, lead a variety of lifestyles. We vary in our faiths, our beliefs, our values, our financial means and our intentions. Many of us share a desire to serve others within our own culture, and also people of other races and nationalities. Service to others is foundational for many cross-cultural friendships worldwide, including ours with you.

Your warm welcome of us and our children affirmed that our love for you is reciprocated. And our discussions with you confirmed that your lives were impacted positively by us too. To hear you talk about the bridge, the coffee cooperative, the many brick houses with iron sheet roofs, and your heightened awareness of working together to solve common problems, was delightful. We felt as if we had seen fruits of our labor, but more than that, we witnessed fruits of the spirit. That's the best kind of fruit!

The personal stories and drawings shared in the student-written books that we brought back to the USA are treasures and will be enjoyed by many American students. We have much to learn from you about living on faith and enjoying the non-material aspects of life.

As we continue with our lives in America, we have peace and joy in remaining connected to Ibanda. Adam and Benjamin now also have that connection. As they grow into adults, they will hold a special place in their hearts for you. I think they will find a way to get back to Uganda one day.

I hope that we will meet again. God bless you and keep you.

Love,
Carrie

The second purpose of this book is to thank the multitude of people who have and continue to serve others. I think of so many expatriates and locals who have served with Habitat for Humanity, Peace Corps, and countless other service organizations. I think of my mother who revamped the "Room in the Inn" program for homeless people at her church in Charlotte. I think of people working with special needs children in the schools. I think of pastors, community health workers, educators, and many others who work for social justice around the world. There are many "Jobs" (grassroots people who are making a difference in their own community) who deserve recognition and thanks.

I smile as I reflect on the array of new friends that we made on our recent trip to Uganda. Stephen, Kirk and Laura, and Jeremy and Tamara– each of their stories is unique and contrasts greatly to each other's service experience. These new friendships are exemplary of connecting dots and being enriched by the intersections.

Stephen, the soccer guy in Ibanda, came from brokenness. A school dropout who worked in night clubs in Scotland, and ended up serving 4 years in prison, Stephen has found the fulfillment of serving underprivileged kids in a rural African village. I hope he will someday write his story.

Stephen has lived in Uganda for two years now. He started with a vision for providing sports opportunities for kids in rural schools that have not even one soccer ball. His organization, Community Development through Sport, serves 12,000 kids (boys and girls) through football (soccer) and netball. His program employs 22 young adults who are not only active in the sports programs but also serve as educators on HIV/AIDs to students and communities throughout the Rwenzori Mountains. He has built the nonprofit through small individual donations and manages his personal life and the sports program on a shoestring budget.

Bob and I were blown away by Stephen's ministry. He doesn't call it a ministry, but Stephen is serving and having major impact on the communities of western Uganda. We are thankful that Adam and Benjamin had the opportunity to learn from Stephen and to see God using a person with such a troubled background to make a difference.

Adam and Benjamin were also thrilled to have the opportunity to spend time with Kirk and Laura and their four boys. Kirk comes from a lineage of American missionaries and he and his wife Laura have been serving as missionaries in Uganda for 12 years. Uganda is home for their children. Travelling to the US to see grandparents and other family is vacation for them. They live the unique life of missionary kids ("MKs"), a life shaped not by where they grow up but by the fact that they grow up in a place so different from the culture of their own nationality. Kirk is the brother of Brent, who with his wife Inell, served as a missionary in Uganda for over 20 years. Our friends Brent and Inell were such an inspiration to me and Bob during our three-year term in Uganda and we have stayed in touch with them through the years.

Jeremy and Tamara are new missionaries to Uganda. We learned about them through friends in our home town. They were living near us before moving to Uganda. We visited them in Uganda to learn about their work and to share a slice of "home." They enjoyed seeing our kid's T-shirts, which advertised our local professional baseball team, the Asheville Tourists, and our nearby high school, AC Reynolds.

We were fascinated with their story. Jeremy explains, "It started with God's call, but no details. When we saw the picture and profile posted of a family serving in Uganda on the internet, we took a step of faith. Having never met them, we emailed the family and asked if we could come live with them to get our feet wet, and to learn the language and the culture. Six months later we had raised enough financial support and we were off to Uganda with Equip International, a mission organization which practices a grassroots approach to serving community needs."

At the time we visited Jeremy and Tamara, they had found their niche as community social workers in Masese 3, a "refugee camp" turned slum where some of the Karimojong Tribe ran from war and famine in northern Uganda 50 years earlier. Jeremy and Tamara are committed to serving an initial two year term and will remain open to God's timing for future placement.

I also have tremendous appreciation for those who serve by supporting the sojourners. We delighted in telling our Ugandan friends that we were only able to come because hundreds of people back home supported us prayerfully and financially. Sharing our journey with family and friends has been a highlight of our past year and has linked us to people in ways we never would have imagined.

One of those connections was with author Frye Gaillard. Through the writing of his book, *If I were a Carpenter: Twenty Years of Habitat for Humanity*, Bob and I came to know Frye, even though I had been familiar with him as a writer for The Charlotte Observer. For his book on Habitat, Frye travelled in 1994 to Uganda, as well as several other countries, to interview staff, volunteers and homeowners about their Habitat experience. Job, Bob and I were among the people he interviewed, resulting in an Uganda chapter of his book.

I had not been in touch with Frye for 12 years. Seeking his address to inform him about my *Portraits of Uganda* exhibit, I "Googled" Frye and was pleased to see all the books he has written since we last met. But I was shocked to see that Frye was scheduled to be in Asheville five days later to speak about his most recent book on Jimmy Carter, *Prophet from Plains*. I contacted Frye and met with him when he came to town, and then again when he returned to see *Portraits of Uganda*. During both visits, Frye expressed interest in helping me "in any way" to write the book because he felt "compelled to be involved."

My reconnection with Frye is only one example of connected dots that have made this book and our mission trip an exciting and rewarding journey. And though Frye and his wife Nancy were unable to make the trip with us as they had planned, Frye's role in this project has been crucial. He has encouraged my writing, pushing me to keep moving forward. He has read my manuscript along the way. We have talked on the phone and he has visited me several times throughout the past year, spending hours listening to my story and giving professional guidance.

To my fellow servants,

Thank you for giving to your family, community, and the world at large. It is only through a collaborative effort that we will make this world a better place. Each drop in the bucket counts. What you do matters, even if you cannot see tangible results. Evil and ill-will lurk around our edges, trying to steal our passion. Hang in there. When you are serving out of genuine desire to help others, whether out of a commitment of faith or not, what you do matters. And sometimes just being there is enough.

Mission, compassion, social and economic justice, and environmental protection are a few of the many causes compelling us to engage. There is a world of need, starting in our own homes, continuing out our back doors, and further into our small towns, large cities and beyond. The needs and opportunities for service are endless. Even broader than the world of need is the diversity among us, the servants, the team players, the body of Christ, the world citizens. We are equipped in different ways to serve different needs. Thank you for matching your gifts and interests with a need somewhere.

My experience – the call, my response, the countries, the circumstances, and the outcomes – are unique to me. My epiphanies however, may look similar to yours. But even if they are different, I'm sure you have experienced personal growth in a powerful way. You probably also have some people buried in your hearts, people who have become part of you, inseparable from who you are today. I hope you will stay connected and continue to seek new opportunities for service that will enrich your lives in new ways. And, I hope you will share your places of transformation with your children and other loved ones.

May God continue to bless you with His grace, His provision, and His protection.

Love,
Carrie

The third purpose of this book is to inspire others to engage in service work. Whether it's in your local Habitat for Humanity affiliate, your place of worship, AmeriCorps, a local nonprofit or an international development agency, the place or time period doesn't matter. I have never heard anyone who has returned from a mission trip say, "I wish I hadn't gone." To the contrary, travelers' responses usually reflect words similar to the college students' we met on the airplane coming back from Uganda. They had spent a month working with farmers in a remote village in Uganda with World Harvest. Their words were, "It was life changing."

Finding "your place" can be challenging. These questions may help you determine where to begin your search.

What experiences have you had that have led to significant personal growth?

When was a time you felt that you made a difference in someone else's life?

When was a time that someone made a difference in your life?

When have you experienced the "peace that passes understanding"?

What hopes and dreams related to service work keep recurring for you?

The best place to start is where your heart is. Past experiences help us identify our passions and what really matters to us. We must choose a focus, either a locale or a cause, knowing that our passions may be different at different stages of our lives. For instance, helping to provide decent shelter was the passion for me and Bob. That focus has shifted to many needs in our local community, where Bob works with a community foundation. And because we are raising children of our own, our passion has grown to include child-friendly service opportunities.

Moving beyond hopes and into the reality of obstacles, I pose these questions for consideration:

What are your fears?

What keeps you from pursuing the adventure you have dreamed of or from answering a call to service?

What hinders you from moving forward?

What blocks the vision you have had for a particular cause?

I offer these words of encouragement. Allow time for the right connections to happen. Your "place" may even lie in your own neighborhood. Listen patiently. Look for dots that are waiting to be connected. Conquer your fears. Cast your net wide. Let go of control. And enjoy watching the magic unfold.

Of course living in rural Africa or other third world location is not for everyone. Don't force yourself into a place or situation that is not a good fit. But don't make assumptions based on your fears either. Don't let low self-esteem or lack of funds steal the adventure that awaits you.

Start where you are. Consider your stage of life and how that affects your timing and place of service. Bob and I talked about our mutual interest in overseas living before we got married; we both felt compelled to serve internationally. From then on, we have taken one step at a time, with each other and with guidance from God.

Our interest in Habitat for Humanity began in 1989, as we volunteered with our local Habitat affiliate in Charlotte, NC. Thirteen years later, we ended 11 years of employment with Habitat at the Jimmy Carter Work Project in Durban, South Africa. The Jimmy Carter Work Project (JCWP), a blitz build week that takes place annually in different locations around the world is for many the pinnacle experience with Habitat. Thousands of volunteers have worked at the 25 JCWPs that have stretched from the Cheyenne River reservation in South Dakota to New York City to the Philippines. At the JCWP in June 2002, hundreds of volunteers from all over the world came together at different locations throughout Africa and built 1,000 houses. At the Durban location alone, we built 100 houses. It was one of the most amazing weeks of my life.

Two personal interactions with President Jimmy Carter made this blitz build most significant for me. Towards the end of the week when we were diligently working to finish our house, President Carter walked in as he was making his rounds, checking for quality and progress. Of course, I wanted to shake his hand and thank him for all the amazing things he has done. But that's not the conversation that transpired. He looked around and said, "You should have painted this room by now."

That was it. He continued on his construction tour, serious about assuring all 100 houses would be completed by Friday. I thought, "He is so not about his own glory. He is truly a servant, living out his faith with action and humility."

The other interaction with President Carter that week was with our children. Many of the HFHI staff had young children who were not allowed on the construction site because of safety issues. Knowing that we certainly could not have missed the opportunity to show our children the Habitat work site, we brought a van of kids to the site after work hours and walked them up the street to show them the houses being constructed. As we rounded the corner to see the next row of houses, we were surprised and excited to see Rosalyn and Jimmy Carter walking towards us.

Jimmy Carter asked, "Who are these children?"

Afraid that we were in violation of policy, the Africa Area Director quickly responded, "These are our children. We are showing them the site and will take them back to the hotel immediately." President Carter reached out his hands and said, "Come children. This is a photo opportunity." We parents pushed our children together with President and Mrs. Carter as we scrambled for our cameras. For me, that special picture holds the memory of a week that is also treasured by thousands of people – volunteers, staff and beneficiaries of Habitat throughout Africa.

For years, I have admired Jimmy Carter and his tireless efforts towards world peace, disease prevention and other significant works of the Atlanta-based Carter Center. His role as a Habitat advocate and the organization's most well-known volunteer has contributed hugely to the success of HFHI. Habitat is now working in over 80 countries and is serving 60,000 families per year worldwide.

I also have tremendous respect and appreciation for Millard and Linda Fuller, co-founders of Habitat for Humanity. Their vision, commitment and life-long service have made an incredible impact on affordable housing worldwide. They conceived and grew a vision of eliminating poverty housing from one small community in Congo (formerly Zaire) to what is now one of the largest house building organizations in the world.

Other famous philanthropists have made tremendous contributions to addressing world needs through their response to a tug in one direction or another. Renowned contributors like singer, Bono of the popular band U2 and talk show host, Oprah Winfrey have brought Africa to the forefront of world concern. Former vice president, Al Gore has also brought awareness and a call to action on global warming issues. Through their celebrity platforms, these committed and concerned individuals have inspired millions to get involved.

But you don't have to be a pop star, a famous TV personality or a well known politician to make a difference. In fact, most change for the better happens through the relationships of ordinary people like you and me. By taking interest in others' lives and connecting the dots, we gain wisdom and fulfillment, and have a lot of fun in the process. Ordinary people do extraordinary things.

I learned this from Job.

Kyanya-Ibanda Bridge
c/o Malighee Job
Kyanya-Maliba S/C
PO box 241
Kasese, Uganda
East Africa

19 August, 2009

Dear Donors,

On behalf of the community, I wish to extend our sincere gratitude and appreciation for the support you have given us for the construction of the bridge. We thank the Lord who gave you the spirit of obedience when Bob and Carrie told you how we needed help, through their experience of three years here in Uganda. They could see the dangers caused by the river. People lost their lives every rainy season. We highly thank you for your contributions and we thank Bob and his family for coming to witness a job well done.

For me and my family, we thank God, who guided Bob and Carrie to join Habitat for Humanity. It was God's plan that they came to Ibanda to help the living conditions in the communities by building better homes and constructing a bridge in the area. They also helped me personally. They trained me how to keep the book of accounts. They helped me to get a good brick house, replacing the grass thatched house my family was living in. They came to know my life history; hence they sympathized with me and my family. Bob and Carrie are my friends who comfort me when they send me greetings. Thank you to their parents for bringing them up well.

I continue as chairman of the bridge committee. We are now raising funds to construct a footbridge, connecting Ibanda to Bikone, a village higher in the mountains. I pray that some of you will take interest in helping our efforts.

May God bless you.

Thanks.

Yours Malighee Job

KYANYA-IBANDA BRIDGE PROJECT
BIKONE PARISH
MALIBA SUB-COUNTY
DATE 19th - 8 - 2009

Fuller, Millard. *Theology of the Hammer*. Macon, GA: Smyth & Helwys, 1994. Print.

Gaillard, Frye. *If I Were a Carpenter: Twenty Years of Habitat for Humanity*. Winston-Salem, NC: J.F. Blair, 1996. Print.

Hope, Anne, and Sally Timmel. *Training for Transformation*. Vol. 1. Zimbabwe: Mambo Press, 1989. Print.

Lindbergh, Anne Morrow, quote - www.people.ubr.com, 30 Jan. 2010. Web.

Mother Teresa, quote - www.quotationsbook.com, 30 Jan. 2010. Web.

Ortberg, John. *If You Want to Walk on Water, You've Got to Get out of the Boat*. Grand Rapids, MI: Zondervan Pub. House, 2001. Print.

Peterson, Eugene H. *The Message Remix (Bible in Contemporary Language)*. New York, NY: Navpress Group, 2003. Print.

Pluth, David. *Uganda Rwenzori: A Range of Images*. New York, NY: Little Wolf, 1996. Print.

Praise You in This Storm, song. Words and music by Mark Hall and Bernie Herm. Performed by Casting Crowns, Copyright © 2000-2007

Randolf, G., quote - www.quotationsbook.com. 30 Jan. 2010. Web.

Stacey, Tom. *Tribe*. New York, NY: Stacey International. Print.

Storti, Craig. *The Art of Coming Home*. Yarmouth, ME: Intercultural Press, Nicholas Brealey Pub., 2001. Print.

Werner, David. *Where There is No Doctor: a Village Health Care Handbook*. Palo Alto, CA: Hesperian Foundation, 1992. Print.

Yeoman, Guy. *Africa's Mountains of the Moon: Journeys to the Snowy Sources of the Nile*. London, England: Elm Tree, 1989. Print.

Yunus, Muhammad, ed. *Jorimon and Others*. Third edition. Dhaka, Bangladesh: Grameen Bank, 1991. Print.

To order additional copies of *Village Wisdom*, visit the website:
www.villagewisdombook.com